CROC!

SAVAGE TALES FROM AUSTRALIA'S WILD FRONTIER

ROBERT REID

ALLEN&UNWIN

Back cover photographs: Ron and Krys Pawlowski (top left), and Ron with his gun and walkie talkie (top right) [photos courtesy Ron Pawlowski]; and Jeff Tanswell [Jeff Tanswell].

First published in 2008

Allen & Unwin
83 Alexander Street
Crows Nest NSW 2065
Australia
Phone: (61 2) 8425 0100
Fax: (61 2) 9906 2218
Email: info@allenandunwin.com
Web: www.allenandunwin.com

National Library of Australia
Cataloguing-in-Publication entry:
Reid, Robert, 1939–

Croc! : savage tales from Australia's wild frontier / Robert Reid.

9781741755800 (pbk.)

Crocodiles – Queensland, Northern. Crocodile attacks – Queensland, Northern. Crocodile hunting – Queensland, Northern.

597.9809943

Internal design by David Thomas
Set in 11.5/16 pt Caslon 540 by Midland Typesetters, Australia
Printed and bound in Australia by Griffin Press

10 9 8 7 6 5 4 3 2 1

CONTENTS

ACKNOWLEDGEMENTS

During the research and writing of this book I spoke to many people about their experiences with crocodiles. Some are mentioned in these pages, but there are far too many to thank individually. Suffice to say, much of the information offered was useful in one way or another, so my appreciation goes to all those who gave their help, advice and observations on the subject of the north's most dangerous residents (certain humans may challenge for that dubious honour, but that's another story!).

Special thanks goes to the shooters and their families who made the adventures of these tough and resourceful men and women come alive.

Among them is the late Vince Vlasoff's daughter Nilla, who shared her memories and allowed access to her father's archives. Thanks also to Ron Pawlowski for our many enjoyable conversations, and to his son, George, who contributed family anecdotes and recollections of his childhood in crocodile country.

I also acknowledge the assistance of George Craig at Marineland Melanesia on Green Island, who gave freely of his vast knowledge of crocodiles, and also the redoubtable

Louie Komsic, whose good humour and toughness knows no bounds.

Thanks to 'Crocodile' Mick Pitman, who recounted his experiences with the legendary 'German' Jack Kiel, and to Jack Sweeney for the true tales of his shooting days around the north of Australia and Papua New Guinea.

Bob Plant's straightforward approach to life and his bush philosophy are hallmarks of this man's no-nonsense character and made our interviews informative and highly amusing—although some of his blunt anecdotes about people and places couldn't be included in this book.

Richard Ralph's observations and first-hand knowledge of the death of his friend Beryl Wruck were invaluable to the chapter on that tragic incident.

Bryan Peach, an author and authority on the subject of crocodiles, was obliging and unselfish with his time and assistance during the writing of this book.

Background on the late Rene Henri was garnered from many sources, including memories and personal stories from those of the shooters who knew him during their time with the Australian Crocodile Shooters' Club.

The late Lloyd Grigg, who is survived by his wife Lyn, was generous with his archival material during his retirement and allowed full use of his extensive photographic collection.

Thanks also to Rob Bredl, the 'Barefoot Bushman' whose knowledge of crocodile behaviour is second to none, for his help during a difficult time with family illness and a bereavement to contend with at the time of writing.

Crocodile attack survivor Jeff Tanswell allowed the author exclusive use of a photograph taken just after his miraculous escape, and professional fisherman Dave Donald supplied a photograph of a mutilated crocodile in the wilds of Cape York.

Finally, thanks to *The Cairns Post* editor, Mark Alexander, for his invaluable assistance.

CONVERSIONS

1 inch		2.54 centimetres
1 foot (15 feet)	12 inches	30.38 centimetres (4.55 metres)
1 yard (50 yards)	3 feet	0.9144 metres (45.72 metres)
1 mile (500 miles)	1760 yards	1.6093 kilometres (804.65 kilometres)
1 acre (4 acres)	4840 $yards^2$	0.404 hectares (1.616 hectares)
1 gallon (44 gallons)		3.7854 litres (166.55 litres)
1 ton		1.016 tonnes

INTRODUCTION

The Far North, particularly Cape York Peninsula, is Australia's last great frontier. It is a region that encompasses such a diversity of wild natural beauty and courageous human endeavour that the very name conjures up a world of adventure, danger and death.

One of the planet's most feared predators, the estuarine or saltwater crocodile, has claimed Cape York as its territory for millions of years, perhaps as long as the land itself has existed. And of the different species of crocodile that inhabit the world's tropics today, the Australian saltwater crocodile is known as the largest and most aggressive. It has remained unchanged during its long reign on earth because of one single factor: it is instinctively a killing machine with immense power and the ability to stalk its prey with deadly patience.

The crocodile has shared its ancient Antipodean homeland with humans for possibly 60,000 years. First came the Aboriginal people, and then, in the 19th century, white Australians gained a foothold as pioneering settlers.

This book tells the stories of brave and resourceful crocodile shooters from the 1940s through to when shooting was finally banned by the Queensland Government in 1974. It also includes horrific crocodile attacks that have resulted in death, and incredible tales of survival against the odds. This was never meant to be a scientific book, but rather a factual account of civilised man and savage beast sharing the same environment.

For the purposes of this book, Cape York Peninsula is that part of north Queensland that stretches in a straight line from about Ingham on the east coast to the southernmost point of the Gulf of Carpentaria in the west. This line takes in the towns of Georgetown, Croydon, Normanton and Karumba—all traditionally included in the general area known as Cape York. Occasionally, references stray south to Townsville, west to Burketown, and north to Papua New Guinea, but such inclusions are critical to the Cape York Peninsula crocodile story.

Out of necessity, the names of crocodile shooters criss-cross each other's stories. They shared the same territory and timeframe, of barely 30 years in many cases. Most knew each other well and they sometimes shared the same paths as they pursued their dangerous profession. Most of them were loners, but there was a bond, a camaraderie among them, forged out of respect and a sense of brotherhood.

There were other crocodile shooters whose stories, for various reasons, are not told in this book. Characters like Henry Hanush, for example, were well known as fearless hunters, and many of them quietly went about their business without fanfare. But they all belong in the roll call of men and women who endured the hardships and dangers of the Peninsula to call themselves professional crocodile hunters.

PART 1: THE SHOOTERS

1 RENE HENRI

The founder of the Australian Crocodile Shooters' Club was not an Australian at all, but a Frenchman—and a woman's hairdresser at that! This most unlikely adventurer was Nice-born Rene Henri, who owned a salon in his adopted home of Melbourne. Despite this rather unmanly profession and his socialite lifestyle, Henri was by nature an outdoorsman and keen shooter, and had adapted well to Australian bush conditions.

In 1947, then in his early 40s, Henri first saw saltwater crocodiles in their native habitat while holidaying at Cooktown. He was immediately fascinated by the fierce animals and returned to Melbourne convinced there was an opportunity to establish a new sport in Australia's northern frontier.

He was back again a year later, determined to learn as much as he could about hunting these dangerous predators.

It was a daunting task, but Henri persisted, and eventually sought out an Italian professional shooter named Guido Juneo, who lived on the estuary of the Annie River, a waterway that flows into Princess Charlotte Bay.

Henri began his search for Juneo at Coen, a one-pub town, 550 kilometres north of Cairns in the centre of Cape York Peninsula. The Frenchman spent a week in the pub, drinking with the locals and getting to know the lay of the land. Years later he wrote how the news spread quickly about the crazy 'frog' who had come all the way from Paris to shoot crocodiles! The truth was, Henri had been in Australia more than half his life and justifiably considered himself a true blue Aussie! Despite the pub banter, he was well liked and soon acquired a great deal of local knowledge that was essential for a stranger in those days to survive. It would have been near impossible to locate Guido Juneo without that knowledge. Even so, it took Henri eight months to make the connection.

Juneo was an eccentric, reclusive hunter who lived rough in a tent campsite, with just two or three Aboriginal helpers to keep him company. Henri described meeting the bushman at his lonely river outpost:

> As we reached the big tent I jumped down [from the truck] in anticipation of meeting my host after months of waiting. I greeted the blond-haired thin man with my best smile and introduced myself, putting out my hand. In return I got a weak handshake and a sulky look! I could nearly read his mind, 'What is this bloody Froggy doing up here?' Perhaps

> he thought I was coming to compete for his skins. He was rather strange! However I had not come to criticise my host, who must have been a loner.

He certainly was. Henri, though, had come well prepared, with plenty of food and hunting gear, including a thousand rounds of .303 ammunition. This placated Juneo somewhat, but he was still suspicious of the French 'greenhorn', whom he obviously considered to be a liability in the dangerous business of crocodile shooting.

Indeed, when Henri first arrived in Cairns he was dressed in a tropical white suit in the style of the stereotypical African 'great white hunter', which drew a lofty comment from the town's newspaper, in which he was described disparagingly as a 'rabbit shooter'. But Henri was far from that, having hunted in the Congo, shot tigers in India and established himself as a crack shot in Australia while hunting wild pig and deer. He proved this at Juneo's camp when the sceptical host put the newcomer to the test by demanding he demonstrate his marksmanship, or, as he put it sarcastically, 'You can show me your skill with your famous sporting rifle.'

Henri later described the scene in a magazine article.

> At daybreak the boys were gone and after a leisurely breakfast Juneo appeared with the smallest tin I ever saw and [said], 'This'll be your target'. He nailed it to the bottom of a tree. I asked for some time to sight my rifle for distance. I knew it was about 75 metres. Also for accuracy. Well, here it was! I felt like William Tell—I could not miss the apple! Raising my rifle to the target with a slow movement

> I emptied the magazine, blasting the target and filling the spot with lead!!!

Juneo's response was a succinct, 'Okay, you'll do, providing you do the same on crocs!'

As a result of Henri's shooting ability, Juneo came to accept Henri as a worthy contributor to his operation. Also, the Frenchman was a keen student and willingly pitched in to help skin crocodiles and prepare the skins for transport and sale by using the 'Juneo Secret Preparation'. Juneo's jealously guarded treatment resulted in his skins being light and dry, 'like cardboard', unlike the conventional arsenic treatment applied immediately to a moist skin, which often resulted in bacteria contaminating and ultimately destroying the hide.

Henri's description of the skinning process vividly portrays the harsh conditions these men endured in the early days of professional crocodile shooting.

> I had brought with me three big curved skinning knives and a stone, as we had to sharpen them every ten minutes or so. Jimmy, the Aboriginal skinner, was a master at the art, quick yet with effeminate hand movements, that incidentally all natives have. He warned me to be careful and not put even the smallest notch in the skin, particularly in the belly of the animal, that being the most valuable part which would reduce it to half its value if damaged. I was amazed that contrary to any other animal I had skinned, crocodile had to be detached from the carcass inch by inch. There was no tearing the skin off. Hence the tedious and delicate work. We were skinning with our feet buried in the

> mud, yet with no human being around the mud was clean. As we worked I conversed with Jimmy and would glance across the river, where invisible sharks and crocodiles were cruising, whilst cat fish came near our toes to pick up bits of flesh we discarded. When the skin was off the animal the inner was snow white contrasting with the outward golden belly and greyish green side. The carcass was slid into the river to feed its own kind! The skin would be hung on a branch in the breeze for sometime whilst we proceeded with more skinning and at the end of the day they would be pinned down with long nails over shady dry ground.

Henri records that the enterprising Juneo ordered his men to 'stretch the skins to the limit to gain extra inches' as the skins were sold to buyers by their size!

Henri's stay with Juneo produced invaluable experience for his future crocodile-shooting enterprise and more than one hair-raising encounter with the giant animals. Once the shooting party camped under the stars on the North Kennedy River estuary, where it runs into Princess Charlotte Bay, not bothering to erect tents as they intended to stay there for just the one night. While Juneo set up his camp bed well away from the shore, Henri decided to take advantage of a breeze nearer the water, tying the four legs of his bunk to a cluster of small trees. It wasn't a good decision. Being close to the sea, the tides moved swiftly and silently through the mangroves. Henri tells the story:

> I was wakened by a terrific noise. It sounded like a tornado going through the trees and I had been thrown out of my

> bed into the water! In full moonlight I could see my bed being dragged away at full speed towards the deep water. I heard a snap as the legs of the bed gave way and were swept away, while the rest of the bed was caught between two trees.

Henri's shouts brought Juneo to the scene and together they moved what was left of his bed to higher ground, where they lit two fires and slept between them 'like Aborigines'.

The next morning the two hunters inspected the scene. 'Well, you've had a visitor,' Juneo said. 'Look at the size of the prints. It was a big one.' It was immediately clear that a large crocodile had approached the sleeping Henri on the rising tide, but had become entangled in the ropes securing the bed, and, fortunately for the Frenchman, became alarmed and retreated back into deeper water.

Another near-miss occurred when Henri and his Aboriginal companion Jimmy startled two sleeping crocodiles while paddling a canoe near a riverbank. The agitated crocs reacted by charging the canoe and veering away at the last moment, almost swamping the vessel. But that wasn't the end of it.

'We had hardly wiped the water of their splashes from our bodies when we heard a noise coming from thick bushes on the overhanging bank,' Henri recounted:

> Suddenly dead over our heads we saw the belly of a huge crocodile flying through the air. The end of its tail just missed the canoe and it vanished in the current.
>
> This was uncanny. It was as if we had crashed in upon a

> crocodile gathering! Waves lurched the canoe so much that I really thought it would turn turtle. I grabbed my gun, but fortunately Jimmy balanced the rocking craft. Juneo had said you never know what can happen with crocodiles and how right he was!

Juneo also taught Henri that 'you can never relax in this part of the world' and that he should 'shoot to kill' without hesitation any time he was confronted by a crocodile. And from then on Henri did just that. The Frenchman recounts how he at last earned the total respect of the redoubtable Juneo while hunting with Jimmy on the North Kennedy River. After killing a medium-sized crocodile, his very first, the two dragged it to shore. Jimmy then departed, leaving Henri to skin the beast and continue the hunt alone.

> I felt like a butcher sharpening my skinning knife. I made sure I had reloaded my rifle and stood it next to me. It was ready for any eventuality. Never has a crocodile been skinned with so much care! Now I could have a bag and wallet made which I had dreamed of all my life!
>
> As the tide was rising I could see small crocodiles swimming under water and feeding on crustaceans or small fish. This, on its own was interesting to see. On the other shore some crocodiles were sunning . . . then my instinct made me part two branches which were blotting my view on my left. Something seemed out of place. The tide had crept up by now and soon I would have to move further up. Having the sun against me I thought I could see a black shadow midst the branches. And the more I

looked the more I thought it looked like the nose of one of those midget submarines which came right into Sydney Harbour during the War! I was debating whether perhaps I was dozing when the mass moved and at the same time I saw that it had been heaved by a powerful back leg.

A crocodile! Could it be the 'Bull'? The famous Bull of the Kennedy? No it couldn't. This couldn't happen to me. It would be ironical that after escaping the best rifles of the territory he would be lying near me!

It was true. The novice croc hunter was face to face with an animal that had eluded death and capture for many years. It was a prize much sought after by the professional shooters of the era—including Guido Juneo!

This was not real. It was too big to be an animal. It was like those antediluvians you see in picture books. In a word I froze. I even controlled my breathing. I checked the wind and luckily I was against it. Then I thought of the carcass lying not far away on my right where I had left it. Soon it would start to decompose and attract the master's attention. Then for half an hour or so I just watched. A very interesting study. I wondered at first why he had heaved and advanced only half a metre at a time. But then I realised that only the shiny grey greenish wet part of his body came out of the muddy water and he would not move till it had dried into a muddy colour.

If he moved across to go to the carcass which would soon be covered by the tide he would discover me! What could I do! I was stuck in the mud. I was just an amateur at this dangerous game and would a .303 bullet do the trick?? His head I now noticed was like armour. I needed an elephant gun!! Hundreds of things went through my mind. And the more I saw of him the more I dreaded him discovering me. Then I took the big decision. It had to be him or me!! I could not rise. It would have attracted his attention. So I extricated one leg from the mud and my knee became a support for my elbow. My muddy rifle would not attract his attention and I could see the 'match box' [the crocodile's brain target] well silhouetted against the sun.

I fired! This was my worst moment—the beast never moved. Usually the jaw lifts on impact and then flops on the mud but this had not happened. It was as if the bullet had missed or not penetrated the 'match box'. I stood and emptied my magazine and saw most of the bullets hitting the water on both sides of his head! However, I reasoned that he would have decamped with my first two 'misses' . . .! I reloaded, to be ready, in case!

I nearly sent an SOS with three more shots. Though no doubt Juneo must have heard the fusillade and at any rate he would arrive sooner or later.

Ten or so minutes later I heard someone crashing through the mangroves and Jimmy appeared. As he saw the crocodile he stopped dead in his tracks, his eyes became white and terrified and without even acknowledging my hand wave decamped from sight back into the mangroves.

This made it worse. Did he see life in the animal!? Was one of his eyes still open!? Then he would only be stunned. It happened, I had heard.

After what seemed like hours the tall shape of Juneo appeared, with Jimmy cautiously behind him. They approached the big saurian from the back and Juneo probed him with the barrel of his gun from the side. Then he looked at his head and called: 'You blew his brain out alright!'

I could have dropped with tension and exhaustion but my mate was walking towards me, his hand extended. 'Congratulations' he said with a grin on his face. This was marvellous. This was unbelievable! And then he added: 'You know, he was really mine!'

Yes, I knew and as a matter of fact it was unfair that a mug like me should have the honours. 'Never mind,' he said, 'now you can shoot with me. I can do with an extra hand.'

The Frenchman who had learned to hunt in the Congo jungle had finally been accepted as a professional crocodile shooter in the wilds of Cape York Peninsula. Guido Juneo, whom Henri described as 'a master of his craft, careful, courageous, strong minded', had taught his pupil well.

Word had filtered out about the Frenchman's crocodile adventures and southern newspapers carried the story in great detail. Back home in Melbourne, Henri was deluged with hundreds of letters from people responding to the news, from 'little boys who wanted to carry my gun, to old ladies who told me off for being so cruel to such gentle animals!'

Henri embarked on a lecture tour, showing film footage he had taken on the Cape and inadvertently discovering a new industry—guided crocodile shooting expeditions for tourists with 'the spirit of adventure'. Henri placed an advertisement in *The Cairns Post* newspaper for a suitable boat to use on his tours and soon selected the *Tropic Seas*, a steel-hulled vessel owned and built by a local engineer, Vince Vlasoff. It was a fortuitous choice, as Henri and Vlasoff went on to become the leading partners in the Australian Crocodile Shooters' Club.

In 1949, Henri and his wife Joan embarked on their first voyage on board the *Tropic Seas* with Vlasoff and his wife Olive. On this trip the Shooters' Club was formed, with the ship's company as foundation members. Henri was elected president, with Vlasoff delegated to look after the club's future members and organise expeditions into crocodile territory. Joan Henri and Olive Vlasoff were the club's first female members.

Henri carefully selected people for his club from a wide range of applicants keen to become crocodile shooters. These hopefuls included a seven-year-old boy who offered to scrub the ship from top to bottom just to see a crocodile, to a retired businessman in his seventies, who wondered if his age would be a handicap! As it turned out, two out of every three applicants were rejected. Henri considered the essential qualities needed were 'good fellowship and a sense of humour, physical fitness, and shooting knowledge and ability'.

Henri then brought the successful applicants together in a relaxed atmosphere over dinner, where he quietly observed how well they got on together. Always a stickler for detail, the Frenchman left nothing to chance.

In July 1950, five new members of the first official 'Expedition Crocodile' of the Australian Crocodile Shooters'

Club left Essendon Airport, Melbourne, bound for Cairns and their first meeting with Vince Vlasoff on board the *Tropic Seas*. The vessel was chartered for six weeks, twice the length of time planned for future expeditions, with an aim not only to shoot crocodiles, but to seek out new territory and experiment with different rifles and ammunition in difficult terrain. The new members were also given practical instructions in skinning and curing, and of course the highly dangerous technique of stalking crocodiles.

The *Tropic Seas* steamed out of Cairns on 1 August, transporting the shooting party north along the entire east coast of Cape York Peninsula to Thursday Island in Torres Strait, down the west coast as far as the Skardon River, and back home to Cairns. On board with Henri and Vlasoff and their wives were fellow club members John Correll, Peter Baillieu and H. Jenkins. Also present were Toby Flinders, the expedition's Aboriginal guide, and deckhand Don Rogers.

The party was split into two shooting teams. Vlasoff, Correll and Jenkins formed one, and Henri, Baillieu and Flinders the other. The novice shooters were required to shoot and kill two crocodiles each, without help, and bring them back to the boat in order to achieve full status within the club. Somewhat tongue-in-cheek, these crocodiles were known as 'graduation kills'.

This was the first of many shooting expeditions into the rugged Cape York Wilderness. These historic trips were recorded on film and still cameras and were the subject of public lecture tours presented to enthusiastic audiences by Henri throughout Australia. As a result, club membership grew rapidly and for eight months of the year (the monsoon, or 'wet' season was excluded) the expeditions set forth with a great deal of attention from the press.

In 1951, an offshoot of the Shooters' Club named the 'Gulf Country Club' was formed under the leadership of Major George Mitchell. Based in the Gulf of Carpentaria township of Karumba, the club organised shooting parties to hunt crocodiles from Land Rover vehicles and boats in the swamps and estuaries of the coast. Legendary Shooters' Club member Lloyd Grigg was the official guide.

But as professional shooting grew in popularity, so too did the numbers of amateur enthusiasts who killed and maimed crocodiles indiscriminately. As a predictable consequence, the crocodile population rapidly declined to an alarmingly low level.

Henri later wrote that not only were crocodiles being shot carelessly by the 1960s, but 'they were speared, netted, snared and many were lost by untrained poachers or would-be shooters, who were the destroyers, as they would catch the easy prey for stuffing or souvenir purposes. These were the murderers, and they nearly destroyed the species.' Professional shooting soon became unprofitable and in the early 1960s the famed Crocodile Shooters' Club was forced to close its doors. It was the end of an adventurous era.

Like many professional shooters of the time, Henri became a committed conservationist, calling for an end to what he termed 'the slaughter of the innocents', so that the threatened species could recover and return to its original numbers on Cape York Peninsula. 'The crocodile will still have the right to exist, in his own country, in his own rivers, and we should be proud to have the *crocodylus porosus*, the best and the last of the antideluvian saurians,' Henri wrote.

The Queensland Government acted in 1974 to officially protect all crocodiles in the state. The shooting era was over. Ironically, Australia's most famous crocodile shooting club had helped bring it about.

2 VINCE VLASOFF

Vince Vlasoff and his boat *Tropic Seas* were the backbone of the Australian Crocodile Shooters' Club in the 1950s and early '60s. Like Humphrey Bogart and the *African Queen*, Vlasoff and his beloved *Tropic Seas* conjured up visions of a world of adventure and danger. In fact, Vlasoff was not unlike Bogart's screen character—laconic and tough, but a gentleman by nature.

Although there were other crocodile shooters before them, Vlasoff, together with Rene Henri and Lloyd Grigg, pioneered the professional safari shooting trips that soon made headlines as Australian big-game expeditions that rivalled those in Africa, India and Asia. Vlasoff, with his trademark pith helmet, was the perfect front man for the Shooters' Club. Handsome and suave, the quietly authoritative skipper handled people as well as he handled his boat. Always friendly and attentive, he nonetheless commanded respect from his crew and the many clients who journeyed with him into the wild rivers and coastal waterways of the Cape.

Vincent Nicholas Vlasoff had a colourful Russian heritage, which included a grandfather who had been sent to a Siberian prison camp for forging passports. His father, Nicholas Max Vlasoff, was an engineer from Irkutsk, a town on the Trans-Siberian Railway route near the Mongolian border, who eventually found his way to Australia on a ship via Vladivostok.

Although he was born in Newcastle in New South Wales, Vlasoff called many towns his home as he moved around the state as a child, in particular the rugged hills and valleys of the Blue Mountains. His father hunted foxes, rabbits, kangaroos and 'anything else that came his way' to make a living during the Great Depression years.

The young Vlasoff was inspired by his father's skill with a rifle and, at five years of age using an old Winchester repeater, managed to hit a plate set up by his father on a fence post. 'My shooting career started with that one shot,' he later said, 'for I was delighted as only a child could be, and treasured the memory for a long time.' But he was 14 before his father gave him a rifle of his own. From then on, he spent as much time as he could at rubbish dumps shooting rats. Watching the 'big rats jump as they got hit' was to the boy 'as thrilling a sport as tigers for the Maharaja'.

Later, Vlasoff talked his way into an engineering job in the Blue Mountains town of Portland, where he spent all his spare time 'wandering about the hills' with his rifle, stalking and shooting foxes. When war broke out Vlasoff was lured with the promise of sunshine and golden beaches to north Queensland. His description of arriving in Cairns by ship could well have been used by a tourism marketing agency to promote the region.

> I was amazed at the contrast this new land presented. Zephyr breezes were blowing, cumulus clouds hung in a tranquil sky with high mountains poking up to block their passage; coconut palms decorated the sea front and their leaves glistened and waved in the breeze.

He soon found work with an engineering firm and on weekends pursued his new-found passion for underwater photography, buying a 10-metre boat and building his own waterproof case to house a movie camera. According to Vlasoff, his hobby—together with his foreign-sounding name—led to suspicions he was up to no good and photographing minefields for the enemy! He was, in fact, investigated by the police, but quickly cleared of any espionage activities.

Vlasoff was in the defence forces until 1944, when he returned to Cairns with thoughts of adventure foremost in his mind. In his absence, and to his dismay, his unattended boat had been wrecked on the reef. Undaunted and bored with shore life, he worked as a deckhand for a Chinese fisherman, working the reefs and rivers along the north Queensland coast. This was the life he had wished for, a 'thrilling experience . . . every day's work was a game, and every fish gave us fun and excitement'. This was the time when Vlasoff encountered his first crocodiles. 'As we netted in the rivers,' he wrote, 'crocodiles would steal fish from the nets, and, occasionally, one would get caught. We were terribly cautious of them, but they were timid and remained very elusive as soon as we tried to hunt them.'

During this period Vlasoff had visions of presenting 'this paradise of sport to the sportsman' and his spare time was taken up with sketching ideas for a 'dream boat' that would suit the needs of big-game hunting and fishing. In 1947, ignoring the fact he could ill afford such a project, he began work on a vessel that would turn his dream into reality. The *Tropic Seas* was born.

Vlasoff and Melbourne man Gordon Bowd, a former customs officer, launched the 14-metre, all-steel vessel a year later. It was the first steel boat to be built in Cairns and locals along the waterfront shook their heads in dismay. 'They said she would sink or rust away, but as an engineer I knew what I could do with steel, and the toredo worm of the tropics would not be able to eat it away as I slept!'

At first the *Tropic Seas* was chartered by excited locals for weekend fishing or sightseeing trips, with the occasional charter voyage up the Cape York coast. Then came the turning point in Vince Vlasoff's career. 'One day a letter was handed to me from a party of sportsmen wishing to go crocodile shooting. This was the type of trip I was hoping for.' The letter was from Rene Henri, the Melbourne hairdresser-turned-adventurer. It signalled the beginning of the Australian Crocodile Shooters' Club.

Vlasoff set about gaining experience before he took on

the big-game venture. With his diminutive wife Olive as ship's cook, he recruited Toby Flinders, an Aboriginal guide and expert bushman, who was recommended by a Cooktown associate. Vlasoff and Flinders proved to be a perfect team and they remained together as close friends throughout the crocodile shooting era.

'He was an excellent seaman and superb hunter,' Vlasoff wrote.

> He taught me how to hunt crocodiles. After being out with Toby, I realised I was a happy amateur who hunted for pleasure while he was a professional who could at any time earn his living in the bush with spear and womera. Every day with Toby in the bush was a lesson. As he was approaching a crocodile, he would fold his arms behind his back and purse his lips. Later, I asked him the reason and he told me it was to stop the smell from under the arms reaching the crocodile and frightening it away. He taught me how to stalk by carrying bushes in front of me, how the wind would carry the odour of the hunter in eddie currents to places one would not consider likely.

Toby Flinders was an essential crew member of the *Tropic Seas* and, as a result, became an integral part of the Shooters' Club's success. In 1952, he accompanied Vlasoff to the first Shooters' Club convention in Melbourne. This was a gala week-long event that drew thousands of curious people—including many of the city's socialites—to a series of functions that included official dinners, luncheons and a massive barbecue that featured '200 gallons' of soup made from a 34-kilogram turtle speared by Flinders in Cape York waters.

The quiet, unassuming tribal elder was reported in a Melbourne newspaper describing the city traffic as: 'Him all the same as ant.' Both men were relieved when it was all over and they could return to their hunting grounds. It was a perfect lifestyle for Vlasoff, not only for professional economic reasons, but for personal recreation as well.

> I was happy in this new occupation. Between taking fishing and hunting parties, I would go back to the rivers to hunt and learn more about the habits of crocs. It was slow work stalking in the mangroves and I developed the technique of shooting from a moving motor boat. This was later named as croc-o-planing by the Australian Croc Shooters' Club and can only be done in well stocked rivers. I would travel up the river at low tide close to the bank with rifle ready almost to the shoulder and steer with my feet, at the same time watching the mangroves for some sign of a croc. Sometimes, you would see a tail or leg or part of the head—sometimes the lot. Occasionally a croc would be buried in the soft oozy mud with the last few fins of his tail, clean of mud, sticking up as a tell-tale sign. This was a fast and exciting sport. I was getting about eight crocs a day—some big, some small. I learnt to be able to hit the smallest target accurately from a moving motor boat.

Vlasoff never tired of his adventurous lifestyle and revelled in the danger and excitement of the Cape York frontier. Olive was no less adventurous, and despite her petite frame, braved many a close encounter with her fearless husband. Vlasoff described one such confrontation with a crocodile as he and Olive rounded a bend in a narrow river.

> My wife was in the front of the motor boat and I was steering as usual. On rounding the bend, I saw a large bull croc facing up the river bank, but with his tail still in the water. A quick look through the binoculars showed that I was in his blind spot, so I went straight at him. Since I could not see his head because his back hid it, I decided on a spinal shot to anchor him.
>
> When we were about 30 feet away, I fired because he heard the engine and was beginning to stir. The shot hit home about one inch to the side of the spinal column and he was barely incapacitated. I drove the motor boat up on the mud right alongside him. I was unable to shoot at him because Olive was in front of me. She fast realised the situation and crouched into the bottom of the boat. In the meantime the croc was getting really aggravated as I had cut his retreat off as well as wounding him. I fired again but failed to stop him. The firing range was now about three feet, and it seemed impossible to use a rifle at close quarters with any success.
>
> The croc, in its endeavour to get to the water, did a complete somersault and clapped its mighty jaws like two planks of timber slammed together. All the excitement was over in about six seconds but it seemed as though time stood still before I finally despatched him after he had turned around. We were covered in mud which was thrown about by his frantic efforts.

Close encounters like this one were stock in trade for the Vlasoffs and their parties of adventure seekers. The names Vlasoff, Australian Crocodile Shooters' Club and *Tropic Seas* soon became irrevocably linked with croc hunting in Cape York Peninsula.

By the mid-1960s, however, Vlasoff, together with Rene Henri and their professional shooting colleagues, realised crocodile numbers were in decline and it was time to hang up their rifles. During an interview in 1967, Vlasoff said the practice of night shooting using spotlights had resulted in a surge of shooters who were able to kill crocodiles more easily and with far less skill than trained daytime shooters. 'At night if you see a pair of eyes in the water you can go up to within 10 feet of him and shoot him,' he said.

> In the daytime it's a different story. He's much more timid. You have to stalk him and he's much more alert. The crocodiles that have survived are the ones that won't look at a spotlight at night and are very cautious. Of course, the average shooter hasn't got the knowledge or ability to go after them.
>
> When we first started hunting in the rivers north of Cairns you could almost say there weren't enough mud banks for the crocs to get on. We would go into the mouths of the rivers that run into Princess Charlotte Bay, rivers like the Kennedy and Normanby, and we'd estimate the croc population at about 20. Today you go there and you are very lucky even to see the track of one.

In those days we could shoot three 12-footers a day. In one trip we bagged 20 in a fortnight, all averaging 10 feet long. Today you would be flat out getting one 10-footer every two weeks.

Spotlight shooters caused havoc. The croc could hold his own until the spotlighters came in. Then it became fashionable for everyone in the country to go and shoot a crocodile. The crocodile population was reduced almost to the point of extermination.

Crocodile mania was alive and well in Cairns until the end of the 1960s, with the Vlasoff family providing plenty of entertaining and colourful stories for the media. It was well known around town that the Vlasoffs kept pet crocodiles in a deep pond at the back of their suburban home, less than five kilometres from the centre of Cairns. In fact, at one time, the lagoon—a former brickworks quarry—was home to about 60 of the saurians. That didn't bother their neighbours, as the Vlasoffs were well liked, and Cairns in the 1960s was a laid-back town that tolerated all manner of different lifestyles and eccentric behaviour.

But that tolerance was tested when 40 of the animals escaped, and, in Vince Vlasoff's own words, 'went to town'. They certainly did. And, like the crocodiles themselves, the media also went to town, with the bizarre incident making news all over the world. Fortunately, they were small crocodiles, but they still created no small amount of panic as they spread out into the suburbs after their 'great escape'. 'You can imagine the pandemonium,' Vlasoff said during a later interview. 'Motor cars ran over them, and the kids were catching them and taking them to school. Women rushed into their houses screaming when they saw crocodiles on their back lawns.' One crocodile was returned to the Vlassofs late at night in a police paddy wagon. Typical of the times, the police were polite and good-humoured over the incident.

Vince and Olive were inundated with phone calls regarding the escapees and eventually rounded most of them up by the simple method of throwing a blanket over each runaway and taking them home. The Cairns City Council was mildly concerned, quickly passing a by-law that limited the number of crocodiles that could be kept as pets in the city area to six only! The council also insisted the Vlasoffs build a 2.5-metre high fence around their crocodile enclosure. According to Vince, that was a good idea as he was more concerned about the safety of the animals than the danger they posed! 'That suited us fine as it gave security to the crocodiles. We regard the fence more for keeping potential miscreants out rather than keeping crocodiles in. But it does keep the crocs at home. We always know where they are!'

In another incident, Olive achieved international notoriety as the Australian housewife who saved a crocodile's life using mouth-to-mouth resuscitation. It wasn't quite like that, but it made a good headline. Olive did indeed save a sick crocodile, a two-metre saltie, by dragging it from the lagoon (into the bathroom) with the help of a neighbour, and massaging its heart region until it responded, first by opening one eye, then the other.

'It was definitely not, as some reports said, mouth to mouth resuscitation,' Olive confessed. When Vince returned home, he was curious, but not alarmed, to read a note on the bathroom door that said: 'Crocodile in the Bathroom. Keep Door Closed.'

Olive recalled once tripping over 'something' on the kitchen floor in the dead of night. A flick of the light switch revealed an errant crocodile that had wandered in though an open doorway.

> We were very fond of our crocodiles and we gave about a dozen of them names. One of the smaller fellows was called Sewerage Jack because that's where somebody found him, and because they didn't know what to do with him, they brought him to us. People must have thought we were mad, but if you treat crocodiles with respect, they won't hurt you.

The Vlasoff household was always a place of wonder and excitement for a small child, as the famous couple's daughter, Nilla Kellermeier, later recalled. 'We always had crocodiles around,' she said. 'It was no different to having a dog. The crocs had free range of the yard, and they were in the pond, but that didn't worry me.'

Growing up, it was normal for Nilla and her friends to join the smaller crocodiles for a swim, to the consternation of many parents. 'The neighbours' kids had to have written permission from their parents before they could go in with me,' she said. 'I guess we did it because we were young and silly. But I don't think it was foolish. Sometimes you take calculated gambles. Dad would not have let us if there was a chance to be taken.'

The Vlasoffs were also prominent personalities in one of Cairns' popular, if somewhat bizarre, annual events, the Crocodile Cup. The event, held in the confines of a tennis court and witnessed by hundreds of spectators, usually featured about 30 crocodiles, separated into two divisions, the big ones and the smaller ones. The Vlasoffs usually entered about a dozen starters from their backyard 'stable'. 'The greatest fun usually comes about halfway down the course,' Olive recounted. 'That's when they either made up their minds that it's high time to go back, or they start trekking sideways, or some of the really big, lazy fellows just go to sleep!'

But the world of crocodiles was not the only highlight in the colourful and adventurous life of Vince Vlasoff. In 1953, in partnership with his crocodile hunter colleague Lloyd Grigg, Vlasoff designed and built the world's first underwater observatory. A year later, the 70-tonne structure was towed behind the *Tropic Seas* to Green Island from its construction site on the shores of Trinity Inlet. The Green Island Underwater Observatory was an immediate success, allowing tourists to observe coral and other marine life in comfort and safety several metres below the water's surface. The observatory is a major tourist attraction to this day.

In 1960, Vlasoff and Grigg opened a crocodile show called Marineland on Green Island. This was later purchased by crocodile hunter George Craig and renamed Marineland Melanesia.

Vlasoff was also a skilled salvage operator and skippered the *Tropic Seas* on numerous salvage expeditions along the north Queensland coast and in the Coral Sea. Most notably, Vlasoff added to his already legendary status in 1969 when he led a scientific expedition that recovered a cannon from Captain James Cook's ship *Endeavour*, lost when the ship struck a reef off Cairns in 1770. Eventually, all six jettisoned cannons were recovered. The *Tropic Seas* also located the *Endeavour*'s anchor, which, after a difficult salvage operation, was removed from its coral graveyard and taken to shore. In 1970, Vlasoff was awarded an MBE for his salvage work.

Among his many other pursuits, Vlasoff helped pioneer the game-fishing industry that attracted international sporting identities to Cairns. As a result, the region soon became renowned as the marlin fishing capital of the world, playing host to celebrities such as actor Lee Marvin and television personality Bob Dyer.

In September 1986, Vince Vlasoff suffered a massive heart attack and died on board his beloved *Tropic Seas*. Olive Vlasoff was tragically killed in February 1997 when a vehicle in which she was travelling hit a large rock on the Bruce Highway south of Cairns. The rock had been deliberately placed there by vandals. Olive, a successful ballroom dancer in her youth, was returning to the city with friends after attending a social dance at Gordonvale. The *Tropic Seas* continues to sail the waters of the Coral Sea and Cape York Peninsula.

3 LLOYD GRIGG

The first real-life Crocodile Dundee was surely Lloyd Grigg. The cavalier adventurer wore a crocodile skin vest he made from a Princess Charlotte Bay monster crocodile 35 years before Paul Hogan scored his screen success with the fictionalised Dundee. The vest became Grigg's trademark and, in his role as a leader of shooting expeditions, made him a focal point for wealthy tourists and big-game hunters. 'The vest wasn't particularly functional but it was a good image for business as a hunting guide,' he later said, with his customary wry humour.

With his dashing good looks and gentlemanly charm, Grigg was the Errol Flynn of the bush in the late 1940s and '50s. He was brave and bold, and his swashbuckling style introduced a new image to the dangerous, dirty and exhausting life of the crocodile hunter.

Grigg was born in 1916 in the Victorian country town of Fairfield and grew up on a wheat and sheep farm where he learned to shoot straight as a boy. His grandfather was renowned as a crack shot, and by 12 years of age young Lloyd was following in his footsteps. The Grigg family history proudly claims that a blacksmith forebear helped fashion Ned Kelly's body armour.

Grigg served his apprenticeship as a cabinet-maker and builder, but adventure called and just after the outbreak of the Second World War he joined the army and saw active service in the Middle East and New Guinea. In the Middle East he was a motorcycle escort and provost (military policeman), but in later years proudly declared: 'I never made a single arrest in three years. I was there to look after the men—not harass them!' Grigg, sporting a gallery of tattoos all over his body, was the last Australian to leave the legendary battleground of El Alamein.

Life back in Australia was far too tame for the former Rat of Tobruk and when he chanced upon an early meeting of the Australian Crocodile Shooters' Club in Melbourne he was in his element. It was with this 'wild bunch of gun-happy blokes' that he made his debut as a crocodile hunter on Cape York Peninsula and went on to become a key member of the famed triumvirate of 1950s croc shooters—Grigg, Rene Henri and Vince Vlasoff.

These were exciting years for the 'gun-happy blokes', and in an era not renowned for its bureaucratic red tape, the three hunters enjoyed a lifestyle envied by many a desk-bound male in Australia's southern cities. On board Vlasoff's

Tropic Seas, or bumping through the bush in 'an old Land Rover and a trailer load of gear', Grigg soon made his name as a knockabout adventurer.

'There were only a few tracks on the Cape in those days, but plenty of crocs,' Grigg said.

> There was a croc every hundred yards up some of those rivers and creeks. We'd shoot all day and then skin and dry them the next day. Instead of carrying big bags of salt around with us we used to cure the skins with powdered arsenic. We got the stuff all over us but we didn't worry about it. I've probably still got plenty of it in my system. We didn't think about poisons or toxins then.

Grigg sold his skins to a Sydney tannery for 'five bob an inch across the girth' and captured smaller crocs alive for the taxidermy industry. He explained the technique used for capturing small crocodiles so they remained unmarked in the process.

> When the tide goes down on those rivers the small crocs are up on the mud banks so we used to put a bullet into the mud right under the chin, which caused an impact that would snap the head back and knock them unconscious. They'd come to and we'd have to kill them without marking them so we'd put them in a bag with a stone and hang it over the side of the boat. They'd take all night to drown.

The professional crocodile hunters had a healthy respect for their dangerous prey. They moved about in a hostile environment, where there was no back-up if things went wrong. A single mistake could prove fatal.

> Crocodiles will inhabit a river crossing or water hole and watch it with infinite patience for anything that enters the water or gets too close—including humans. They'll watch you go down for your water day after day, and they'll move a bit closer each day until they judge the time is right. Then they'll be out of the water and at you. I've seen full-sized bullocks pulled off their feet by crocs grabbing them on the snout and rolling over to unbalance them. When that happens it's all over.

Grigg admitted he and his hunter mates would sometimes cool off on a hot day by swimming in the rivers—until they eventually decided it 'wasn't a very good idea'. 'It was a stupid thing to do, but we got away with it, probably because in those days crocs associated humans with gunshots and became wary of us.'

Because white Australians were relatively small in number on the Cape, few were taken by crocodiles. According to Grigg, it was a different story with Aborigines.

> I've been given information from police files that up until 1950 about 60 people, mostly Aborigines, were taken by crocs. Some of them went missing and were never seen again. Aboriginal people never get lost, so you'd have to say crocs got them. Crocodiles, for some reason, seem to like anything black. Wild pigs are usually black, and I used to have a black dog called Nigger which would stand in the

> bow of the boat and attract the crocs. As they came out, the dog would back off and we'd shoot the crocs and drag them into the boat.
>
> But whenever we made camp, that dog would approach the river or creek with the utmost caution. He'd drink, back off up the bank and take a good look around before drinking again.

Grigg emphasised that shooters always tried to minimise the risks inherent in their profession, but danger was always close by and couldn't be eliminated.

> Every croc we harpooned would dive and roll on 50 feet of cable in about five seconds. Then they'd roll back the other way. You would have to pull them up and shoot them through the ear. If you didn't do that, they might suddenly come to in the boat. When that happened—a live croc in the boat—you didn't know whether to dive over the side or take your chances on board. Not much of a choice!

Grigg said he occasionally tackled 'five-footers' in the water with his bare hands—but only 'when I had to! As long as you grab them right you'll get away with it, but you've got to hold the jaws together to stop them opening, otherwise they'll slash you with their teeth right away. I've been snapped at many times, but never bitten.'

Grigg was leader of the 1951 Australian Crocodile Shooters' Club expedition to Cape York when he experienced a near-miss he never wanted to repeat. The expedition was shooting on the Bizant River and Grigg had shot a 'monster' on a mud bank. He leapt into the knee-deep mud and staggered across to the animal, resting his rifle against the huge beast. Suddenly, the 'dead' croc opened its eyes and jaws. 'Shoot the brute!' Grigg yelled to his mates on the boat, but his rifle was blocking the target area. In desperation he grabbed the rifle and expedition member Ted Pearce, a holidaying policeman, put two bullets in the croc's spine.

It took four hours to tow the crocodile back to the *Tropic Seas*, but the launch's cargo winch couldn't lift it onto the deck. The crocodile was measured at 15 feet 4 inches in length.

While Grigg—like his counterparts—admitted the 'old days' were 'open slather' on crocodiles, he said professional shooters didn't blast away at anything that moved.

> We were always welcome on any station or property we visited. It was only later on that shooters started blasting away at cattle and windmills, and all that sort of thing. I think the advent of four-wheel-drive vehicles had a lot to do with it, too.
>
> In retrospect, I think government protection for the crocs was a good thing, although there were always many inaccessible rivers and waterholes where they were quite safe.
>
> We didn't think about whether we'd shoot them out or not, but I do remember Vince saying to me: 'One of these days we won't have any crocs left to shoot'.

Grigg retired from professional crocodile shooting in 1954 to concentrate on other business interests, including the Green

Island Underwater Observatory he built with his partner and friend, Vince Vlasoff, followed by the crocodile sanctuary, Marineland, in 1960. He also developed skills in both still photography and cinematography and is responsible for thousands of photos and rare documentary footage that portrays life as experienced by the crocodile shooters.

In 1986, after many years in retirement, Grigg admitted the lure of adventure was still strong. 'Yes, I miss those days, but the bones get a bit stiff and slow you down,' he said. 'I still *think* I could do it—the mind is still willing!'

On 20 February 2003, Lloyd Grigg died, aged 87 years, in Bundaberg, Queensland. He shot more than 700 crocodiles in his career.

4 G.J. (GEORGE) CRAIG

Whenever crocodiles are talked about across the frontier lands of northern Australia and the wild regions of Papua New Guinea, the name G.J. Craig is certain to be prominent in the discussions. Craig shot and trapped the fearsome beasts in an adventurous career spanning 45 years in some of the world's most inhospitable terrain. If it's saltwater crocodile country, George Craig has been there, and—if the animals were big and bold enough—he's bought 'em back alive.

Since 1972, Craig and his wife Shirley have showcased the 'man-eaters' on Green Island, an idyllic coral island off Cairns. Originally a small oceanarium built by Vince Vlasoff and Lloyd Grigg, the tourist attraction was transformed by the Craig family into Marineland Melanesia, a wildlife park and natural history museum that houses a vast collection of Papua New Guinea carvings and artworks. But it's the monster saurians the tourists come to see, and the star attraction is the mighty Cassius, a 5.5-metre cantankerous beast that weighs in at more than a tonne and is estimated to be 100 years old.

Famous for his scars, evil temper and sheer size, Cassius reigns as the largest crocodile in captivity in the world today. With a piece out of his lower jaw, part of his tail and left foreleg missing, plus a mutilated right foreleg, Cassius is a formidable sight. Despite his age and injuries, the crocodile is alert, active and dangerous.

George Craig knows all too well how dangerous all crocodiles are—especially a veteran like Cassius.

> I have a great respect for him. I know he will give no quarter and you must realise this. Even if you spend many years caring for a croc, even from birth, there may come a day when your foot passes too close to his mouth, and bang! He's got you. It would be your own fault. A croc is a croc. He doesn't show much affection for his owner.

Cassius has another claim to fame. Craig is convinced his mean-tempered charge is Sweetheart, the legendary saltwater crocodile that terrorised fishermen and tourists in the Northern Territory during the 1970s.

Sweetheart was renowned for attacking small boats on the Finniss River, south-west of Darwin, reputedly because the noise of outboard motors disturbed him in his peaceful habitat. It's believed he attacked at least 15 boats, but Territorians claim the figure is much higher because some fishermen were simply too embarrassed to report their encounters, fearing ridicule in the media.

In 1977, wildlife rangers finally trapped a large crocodile they believed was Sweetheart, but the animal drowned during the attempts to subdue and capture him. The crocodile was subsequently stuffed and donated to the Northern Territory Museum, where he remains exhibited as the rogue named Sweetheart.

But Craig is having none of that, and maintains that much evidence exists to support his claim that Cassius is, in fact, the real Sweetheart. For a start, he says, the museum crocodile is smaller than Cassius and has no visible injuries.

> The stuffed croc in Darwin is only 16 feet 10 inches and has no scars at all. It just doesn't add up. With his tail complete, Cassius would be a true 18-footer and there aren't many of those around. His injuries are consistent with Sweetheart's recorded attacks on boats and his aggressive behaviour makes him the meanest crocodile I have encountered. He gets agitated when he hears a marine engine. He's Sweetheart, all right.

Cassius was also captured in the Finnis River, home of the cranky Sweetheart. Experts agree it is not common for two large crocodiles to inhabit the same stretch of waterway.

Cassius was caught in a rope trap by a six-man team that included crocodile specialist Dr Grahame Webb in 1984, and kept in the Northern Territory's Letaba Crocodile Ranch until 1987, when Craig heard about the animal and bought him for $10,000. Webb said the crocodile was one of the biggest he had ever seen. 'Crocs don't get much bigger than that—and he was missing part of his snout and tail.'

It was thought the animal was to be used in a film called *Dark Ages*, but Cassius proved to be far too aggressive and dangerous for the project. Craig and a tough group of assistants hauled the giant beast across the top of Australia in a hired truck. It was a marathon 2500-kilometre journey, with Craig constantly checking the crocodile's condition and keeping him damp and cool. The hunter said transporting crocodiles requires patience and expert knowledge of the animal's physiology: 'Catching them is one thing, but getting them to your destination is another thing. If you don't look after them they can stress out and die.'

After 20 years in captivity, 'King' Cassius still reigns as the boss crocodile among the 50 other saurians at Marineland Melanesia. 'He's in terrific nick,' Craig said.

> This bloke might last another 10 or 20 years. He's still active and he can still jump. The other day he jumped the gun and came up for his food at the fence before I was ready and snapped his jaws about 4 inches from my head—that's 7 feet out of the water! If I had a million dollars I'd build him a huge pool, but then you'd never see him. This place suits him down to the ground. Cassius is living a good life.

George Craig's life reads like a classic 'boy's own' adventure story. Born in Peru in 1930, the young Craig showed an early fascination for reptiles and at nine years of age his father gave him several baby alligators as pets. 'That was wonderful but the gesture ended in disaster,' he said. 'I put them in the bathtub but unfortunately turned the wrong tap on and killed them all in boiling water! But I always kept snakes and lizards and had a talent for handling them.'

Craig soon discovered he had another passion—travelling—and after studying art in London in 1948, embarked on an adventurer's life that led him to fishing in the icy waters of the North Sea, creating headlines as a stowaway on an ocean liner bound for the West Indies, and performing as an aquatic stuntman with Olympic swimmer and *Tarzan* movie star, Johnny Weissmuller.

> That was in the Earls Court Aqua Show in London, an indoor spectacular that was very popular at the time. I was a bit of an all-rounder, a kind of stunt artist, and did comic diving and underwater Houdini-type escape acts. The money was good and I was able to save the 46 pound fare to Australia.

Craig arrived in Melbourne in 1951 and went to work as a labourer on a building site. Before long he heard about a meeting to be held by a group of sports shooters interested in crocodile hunting. Always inquisitive, the idea appealed to the young wanderer, so he invited himself to the meeting! 'I walked in and made myself known, but everybody just glared at me. It wasn't a very encouraging start!' Craig had inadvertently stumbled upon a gathering of the Australian Crocodile Shooters' Club, which had already made its name in north Queensland as a fearless group of professional hunters. 'I was just a young fellow, all enthusiastic, I didn't have any idea who they were,' he said. 'I remember Lloyd [Grigg] was friendly and very positive, and I got on very well with him. Vince [Vlasoff] was the other way, a bit sceptical, as if he was trying to turn me off having a go myself.'

Soon after, Craig hitchhiked to Gladstone on Queensland's mid-north coast and talked himself on board a yacht about to sail to South Australia. It was a 74-day 'journey through hell' that Craig said he was lucky to survive. Too late, he found himself on a vessel with no motor, no radio and no dinghy. And an inexperienced skipper to go with it.

> We were learning as we went along and in places the seas were unbelievable. At one stage we tacked backwards and forwards all night and at daybreak we were still in the same place. Off Victoria we ran into this huge storm and we didn't know where we were for 10 days. I calculated we should have drowned four times during the trip!

Craig earned 20 pounds for the journey, and after a spell in an Adelaide Salvation Army hostel (one shilling a night), he bought a .303 rifle and teamed up with two other drifters, deciding to hitchhike through the centre of Australia and try their luck crocodile shooting in the Northern Territory.

It took them a month, jumping trains and walking up to 50 kilometres a day in searing heat. 'It was hard to get a lift in those days. It was just after the war and there were a lot of tough guys around and you had to be very careful. One time we shot a bullock to survive, and another time an emu, but mostly we lived on black cockatoos.'

Arriving broke in Darwin, Craig worked in a variety of jobs, shooting crocodiles on weekends. After three years, he had enough money to buy his first boat, the *Mangrove Queen*. From then on, Craig was a professional crocodile hunter. It was a hard, tough life, among hard, tough men—some of them highly dangerous. One such character was Ginger Palmer, a notorious knockabout with a penchant for violence and no apparent fear of death.

> I met him first in 1951, when I first started shooting, at his camp at the Forty-Seven Mile, south of Darwin. He was a real wild bugger who'd sit up all night talking about his escapades across the north. He told me he pinched a boat with two other blokes in north Queensland, but overheard them plotting against him, so he killed them and threw their bodies overboard and sailed to Dutch New Guinea.
>
> He was trigger happy and he'd shoot cattle just for fun, not just one for food, but two or three and leave them to rot.
>
> Anyway, we'd shoot crocs from a canoe. We'd paddle along a bank at low tide until we saw a track going up into the scrub and bang the side of the canoe. The next thing a croc would come flying down and if you were lucky you'd get him. We'd pull them alongside and get a hammer or axe and belt the hell out of them. There were some big crocs around, but a lot had been shot before I started.
>
> Ginger had another camp at Gun Point, at the mouth of the Adelaide River. He married an Aboriginal woman from Melville Island, just across the water, but he got very abusive and violent when he was drunk. Not an easy bloke to like. He ended up in Fanny Bay Jail, so the story goes.

In 1956, Craig went to New Guinea crocodile shooting and eventually set up a trading store at Daru, near the mouth of the Fly River. For the next 16 years he hunted crocodiles deep into the Fly River and hinterland waterways.

> I'd go upriver five times a year on 1200-mile round trips while my wife Shirley looked after the store. I went down to Cairns in 1963 and bought a boat called the *Janis B*, which was in the hands of the receivers. I wasn't familiar with the sailing route up the Queensland Coast at the time so I went down to the Cri [the Criterion Hotel on the Barbary Coast, Cairns' notorious waterfront district] and got onto Dusty Jarvis, a well-known bloke who never washed, went barefoot and wore a skipper's hat. Well, I got him off the grog and we sailed up to Thursday Island and I was right then.
>
> The best night's shooting I had was 47 crocs, because they hadn't yet worked out what was happening. You'd go back the next day and there was another lot, providing the tide was out. They weren't all a spectacular size, but they all meant money and you had to make a living. But in Lake Murray we'd get five or six that were too big to get into the boat. If a storm came up at the wrong time you were in danger of sinking.

Like all the hunters from that era, Craig went about his business without too many thoughts about the dangers of his profession. But they were always there, and one careless move could mean a sudden and horrifying death:

> I had a close shave in broad daylight when we were deep in swampland way upriver on the Fly. We were pushing through long grass when my harpoon boy tapped me on the shoulder, saying 'Look . . . look' and pointing ahead of us. I looked up and there was this croc about 16 or 17 feet heading towards us. I wasn't too bothered, because they always turn away and disappear when they realise a boat isn't food. But he kept coming, and he increased his speed to flat out, with a big bow wave. This was most unusual so I grabbed the rifle and stood up in the dinghy. The croc gets to about 10 feet away and he's big and mean and I'm really packing it. Before I can pull the trigger he dives under the dinghy and he's gone. Never saw him again. He didn't even scrape the dinghy. He must have come to the point when he realised he had made a mistake and he'd better get out of the way.

In 1967, Craig captured a notorious man-eating crocodile he had been trying to trap for 10 years. Nicknamed Oscar, the crocodile had terrorised local tribes along the upper reaches of the Fly River and was known to have killed several people.

> I had been warned to be very, very wary of this croc because he had a bad reputation and he was very elusive. I finally caught him in the mouth of the Mipan River, which is off the Fly River, about 500 kilometres north of Daru.
>
> I harpooned Oscar and transported him downriver to my base without injuring him. I never used tranquillisers and I take great pride in catching reptiles without harming them. It takes many, many years experience to capture crocs

> the correct way. You don't pull hard on the harpoon because it will come out, so you have to gradually get closer and closer until eventually you get a snout rope on and secure him, being very careful you don't restrict the flow of blood, or cause him undue discomfort on the journey home.

Oscar measured 'somewhere between 17 and 18 feet' according to Craig. The exact measurement was never recorded, owing to the animal's moody and unpredictable behaviour. 'Oscar was never that keen on being measured so I didn't press the point, but he was recorded in the *Guinness Book of Records* as being the biggest crocodile in captivity at that time.'

Craig kept Oscar at Daru for five years before he became the star attraction at Green Island in 1972. Oscar died in 1987, the same year as Cassius arrived from the Northern Territory. Craig believes the crocodile died from stress, as a result of the construction of a nearby resort on the island. 'Over 800 pylons were driven into the ground at the time, and that's a lot of thumping and vibration. An expert from the United States came over and said it was a very common thing in alligator parks for reptiles to die when there is a lot of building going on. That's why Oscar got stressed out and died on me.'

Oscar, like his successor, Cassius, was a 'problem' crocodile, an animal to be treated with extreme caution. He was a dedicated loner who didn't tolerate company—even from the opposite sex. 'He never accepted captivity and never lost his aggressive behaviour,' Craig said.

> I tried to introduce him to females, but he promptly forgot what they were all about and ate them. I had one very good

> female that he showed some interest in but then he grabbed her across the pelvis and wouldn't let go. I jumped in with a bamboo pole and whacked him over the head until I could rescue her. She had a few broken bones but survived.
>
> Oscar never forgot that incident and I could tell from the mean look in his eye that he would kill me if he got the chance. I never lowered my guard around him. He was like Cassius. One false move or miscalculation and I've had it—it's as simple as that.

With the best part of six decades' experience hunting and handling crocodiles both in the wild and in captivity, George Craig has simple advice to any unwary or foolhardy person who decides to risk a close encounter in crocodile territory.

> A crocodile is a hunter with his own area to patrol, and that may be one end of a river to the other. Anything that moves in his territory is food, and that includes people. If you're in crocodile country, don't go in the water, it's as simple as that. He'll eat you if he gets the chance.

Craig has no regrets about his crocodile shooting and trapping career. It was, he says, an era that allowed adventurous men and women to make a living with a minimum of interference from government officials and bureaucrats.

> But that all came to an end in New Guinea in the early 1970s when it became fashionable to label us 'exploiters of the natives'. What a lot of rubbish! It was a very hard life, and after 16 years I came away with $30,000, which came from the sale of my house and boat. I had to borrow money

in Cairns to get set up again. If I exploited the natives I certainly didn't make much money out of it. Those accusations were very hard to take, but there was a lot of bad feeling against us, so it was time to leave.

It was also the end of crocodile shooting in Australia and by 1974 the practice was outlawed by government legislation. The fearsome crocodiles were now a protected species and it was time for G.J. Craig and the small band of professional shooters to hang up their guns.

It was over.

5 BOB PLANT

Bob Plant was 11 years old when he shot his first crocodile. It was 1940 and Bob was with his father, Bob Plant Snr, in a dinghy motoring up the Nassau River on the western coast of Cape York Peninsula. Young Bob had been out bush with his father many times before and was already a sharp-eyed shooter, but his experience was limited to smaller game, while Bob Snr took on the kings of the Cape—the feared saltwater crocodiles. The Nassau is deep in croc country and in those days crocodiles ruled the waterways, free from predators—except for a small, but growing, band of human hunters. Plant described his first saltie kill:

> We were almost past him with the outboard going when I spotted him asleep on the river bank. Dad shut the motor off when I pointed, mad with excitement, at the croc.

> Without thinking I grabbed Dad's rifle—a 1920 model .300 Savage it was, and jumped out of the boat, bolted up that 10-foot bank like a rabbit and got that croc first shot. He was a nice 8-footer and I was very proud. Suddenly, I was a croc shooter!

He was indeed. Bob Plant went on to become a legendary crocodile hunter—a distinction that only a few of the Cape York shooters can lay claim to. Over the years there were many shooters, but only a small number were truly professional, and of those merely a handful stood out as exceptional.

Plant's father was a tough-as-nails, no-nonsense bushman who had been hunting and fishing in Queensland's wild north since the 1930s. In 1947, he started the first professional safari expeditions into the rugged Cape and Gulf of Carpentaria regions. For the next 10 years his Gulf Sport-ing Tours enterprise became synonymous with outback adventure—a shooting and fishing odyssey that held the promise of a trophy to hang over the fireplace back home. And the adrenalin-charged thrill of danger ever-present in what was then an untamed land. There were fierce boars, giant gropers, sharks and abundant wild duck and geese to hunt and shoot, but the biggest prize of all for the paying customers was undoubtedly the saltwater crocodile. Bob Plant Snr's slogan on his brochures, 'Shoot Your Own Trophy and I Will Cure and Stuff it for You', said it all, and attracted shooters from across Australia, with a sprinkling of international big-game hunters.

'When Dad first started shooting back in the 1930s there were no professional shooters and no market for skins,' Bob said.

> He did it for fun. He just brought the crocs home to look at and they went rotten in the shed! It was a sport back then, and nobody thought there was any money in it. Dad didn't start skinning crocs for money until about 1948.
>
> Dad was a teetotaller, just like me! Most of those fellas lived hard in the bush and would drink hard as well, usually whiskey and plenty of it! But my body would never accept the smell, let alone the taste. Back when Cairns Draught beer was around I'd occasionally have one, but only 50–50 with lemonade. That was the nicest drink going, but if I had two I'd want to go to sleep!

Plant said that danger and death always lurked nearby in crocodile country.

> You know, it doesn't matter how small a creek is, don't think there's no crocs in there, and if there's just one, he'll see you 24 hours before you see him, and he won't take his eyes off you. They are phenomenal how they see, hear and smell you. He'll back in under the mangroves, and he'll lay there and watch you . . . and watch you . . . and watch you. And he'll get you if you're careless.

Versatility and bush ingenuity were the keys to survival in the rough-and-tumble life of a crocodile hunter. Bob built his own shooting dinghies, always constructed from plywood, 'easy to load on to vehicles and quiet in the water', and even built his own truck from surplus army parts left over from the Second World War.

> I assembled the whole thing from scratch, every bolt and nut, without an instruction manual, and did thousands and thousands of miles through the bush in it, just using a compass and army survey maps. You'd get bogged and have to dig yourself out or stay there forever. Once I was stuck up to the axles for several days, three I think, using a timber jack and logs cut from the bush to get out. I still shot and skinned crocs while I was there, though!

Bob used many firearms during his shooting days, from the .308 BSA night-shooting rifle—'not the nicest looking rifle, but a good featherweight'—to the heavier American-made Weatherby MKV 240 Magnum Deluxe. 'I bought that one in '68 and they stopped making that model soon after. It's a beautiful rifle. I don't think I shot a croc with it, but a crow's not too safe at 250 yards away! I had a Winchester .264 Magnum that I really liked as well.'

But Bob never used the .22 rifle favoured by freshwater crocodile shooters and some of his saltie mates. 'They were a damned nuisance, probably good on occasions for 3- or 4-foot crocs, but every time you moved on a boat there'd be salt water splash over everything and those rifles tend to rust.'

Apart from rifles most shooters also carried handguns, and Bob was no exception. He and his long-time shooting partner, Bill Weare, often used these firearms to finish off wounded crocs.

Bill had a 9mm German Luger and I had a .38 Smith & Wesson army issue, both pretty handy guns, but the Luger has more punch. You might have a cranky croc on the end of a harpoon, so if you can get in close you put the Luger right on his ear, and boom!

Bill carried the Luger in a holster. He was always oiling and polishing it, because the salt water turns everything rusty. High quality steel doesn't mean a damn. Take your eyes off the gun for a minute and it turns rusty! Our weapons were always loaded, with the safety catch on. One day, after about six weeks shooting, we were camped at Topsy Creek, and Bill was practising quick draws with the Luger. I'd just cleaned my .38, put the six rounds back in, and out the corner of my mouth I muttered 'I'll show you a quick draw!' and the gun went off! The bullet went through a pile of croc skins and luckily not Bill. The skins were ruined and cost us a lot of money, but I could have shot Bill dead right in front of my eyes!

Plant and Weare spent many years together in an era when the only rules were the ones the shooters made themselves. Shooters depended on each other, not only to survive, but to ensure they brought home the skins to provide them with a living. Crocodile shooting was, after all, a business.

Every day was a new adventure and there was an open-minded 'take it as it comes' attitude common among shooters—a philosophy that was essential for living and working in the harsh Cape York environment. One of those adventures could well have cost Plant and Weare their lives, had it not been for their hardy bushcraft skills. Camped on an isolated riverbank they ran out of fresh water and set out across country searching for waterholes in the desolate country.

> We got lost that night and I was carrying a dead rifle after shooting a brown snake and several wild pigs. Well, we finally found a waterhole, beautiful water, so Bill and I half-filled our kerosene drums and headed back towards camp. That's what we thought, anyway. It was dark and we got lost in the mangroves. We followed a ridge until I saw a burnt tree, still smouldering, that I recognised. A big fire had gone through the area about a week before and the whole Gulf was covered in smoke. I said to Bill: 'We passed that bastard this morning!' Bill thought I was mad, but sure enough, there were our footprints in the ashes. We'd gone around in a big circle! We had to turn around and go back, still carrying these bloody heavy kero tins of water! We found the boat at about midnight. We were completely buggered.
>
> It's easy to get lost up in that country. There are hundreds of river arms that all look the same and you don't know where you are. The tide will rush up one arm, hit another arm, and then it'll be running the wrong way. It's mind boggling. I will never, ever forget that night.

Fresh water was always a precious and scarce commodity, one that croc shooters didn't take for granted, but there were times when they had to make do with a less than perfect drinking supply.

> When water got a bit low we'd mix salt water with the fresh, 20 per cent salt to the fresh. Not nice when you haven't got fresh water! I've seen us drink water that would kill most people—water that cattle and pigs have shit in, trucks gone through it, but I don't think any of us ever got crook from it. I've scooped water up out of two inches of mud and put it in a tin until you've got a couple of gallons and then you'd drink it. What passed through you wasn't normal, but you had no choice! Call it a miracle, call it good luck, I don't know, but we didn't get sick!

In the 1950s, crocodiles were numerous in the many rivers and waterways of the Cape and shooters were limited only by the size of their boats and the time they had to skin the animals.

> In the mouth of the Coleman River one night we shot 16 small crocs up to 7 feet long and I said to Bill don't shoot anything over 15 feet going home, 'cause we had enough to skin the next day. Anyway, there was this big bloke on the river we'd seen a dozen times but could never get. Night after night we passed him but could never get near him. This night he insisted on stopping to have a closer look at us, so we did the right thing and shot him! We had to get a rope on him and tow him half a mile back to camp 'cause the boat was dangerously overloaded. He was a lovely croc, about 14 foot.

In one night's shooting spree on the Kendall River in 1953, Plant and Weare shot 23 crocodiles from Bob's boat,

Heatherbelle, including two well over 4 metres in length. 'That night was a shooter's paradise, almost as if the crocs had lined up to commit suicide,' Plant said.

> But we paid for it the next day when we had to skin and salt them in a race against time before they started to go bad in the heat. It was 10 o'clock at night before we finished. We promised each other 10 crocs a night would be our limit from then on!
>
> Real hot weather and croc skins don't mix. One hour of hot sun on a croc's skin after you shoot him can bugger that skin.

A crack shot, Bob perfected techniques that enabled him to stalk and close in on his prey to make the kill.

> There's only one place to shoot, right in the brain box, from any angle. Just smash the brain and they're dead. Sometimes they'll roll over, depending on what's decomposing in the body.
>
> At night you can see a croc's eye glow, but you can't tell how far away it is, and sometimes it isn't a croc at all! The nightjar bird has a red eye almost as bright as a croc's. You'd sneak the boat up thinking it was a croc and there would be this bloody bird sitting on the bank. Your eyes would be popping out from concentration and you're set up with the rifle ready and it's a bird!
>
> A croc's eye is almost always never the same intensity. Some nights they are as bright as a bright star in the sky, other times they are not so brilliant because he might have

his windscreen over his eyes and they go dull. A freshwater croc's eye is always a flat red. When you get in the upper part of a river you'd see 20 or 30 freshies in the spotlight, but you're after salties because they're worth a lot more, then suddenly a bright star pops up in the water and boom! you've got him. It's funny, but when he's swimming at almost any angle only one eye is shining. I never worked that one out.

Another bird that inhabits the wilds of northern Australia is the great-billed heron, also known to bushmen as the 'giant croc bird' or the 'alligator bird'—alligator, or 'gator', being the widespread term for the saltwater crocodile in the first half of the 20th century. This particular heron stands 1.5 metres tall, has a wingspan of up to 2 metres, and has a frightening, guttural roar that has been mistaken for a crocodile's call. The bird's habitat is restricted solely to northern Australia's crocodile country of coastal lowlands, mudflats and estuaries. Elsewhere, this shy and solitary bird is found in Papua New Guinea and parts of south-east Asia. 'You can hear this extremely loud bellow a mile away at sunset, but it's a bird, not a croc! That yarn is a complete fallacy—one of those stories that once started you can't correct.'

Plant confirms what every crocodile shooter knows—a crocodile will eat anything that moves in the wild, and is particularly fond of dogs, domestic or otherwise. But he and Cliff Walker were flabbergasted one night after shooting a '10-footer' crocodile while camped on the southern bank of the Mitchell River. As the two men hauled the dead animal from the water it belched and disgorged the perfectly preserved body of a cat!

> It was a beautiful golden colour and it didn't have a tooth mark or a blemish on it. Its eyes were open and its ears were pricked. It was very strange. All the feral cats you will see up there are smokey grey, their natural colour. I have never seen a golden cat in the wild. The acids in the crocs stomach must have changed the colour of the cat, if that's possible, I don't know. How fast that croc must have been to catch that cat unaware, whether it was on the bank, or a limb, or wherever. Uncanny.

Plant was also a pilot and often used a Piper single-engine aircraft to 'spot' for crocodiles over the rivers and estuaries of the region. Bob's technique was to zoom over the waterways at '200 feet' and mark the location of crocs for an overland trip later.

> I've flown all over the Gulf and the Cape looking for crocs, or we'd land on the salt pans, taxi right up to the water, and camp for a night's fishing! The last plane I had anything to do with was an American kit plane I paid a bloke 10 grand to assemble for me. It had a German engine and after 40 hours both magnetos failed and I had to come down on a rock cutting the other side of Archer Creek. That partly wrecked it and I sold the rest. It's still around somewhere.
>
> In those days from the air you'd see 10 or more big salties on the bank together, but you'd never see that today. One time I saw two crocs in a lagoon guarding a dead cow

> floating in the water. The big fella was about 14 or 15 feet and the smaller one around 10 feet. Then there was a nest of about a dozen little fellas there as well. It was only a small lagoon too, way up in the Mitchell River. Well, we couldn't fly around there all day 'cause we were a long bloody way from home, so I marked it on the map.
>
> Cliffy [Cliff Walker] and I went back in a 7-ton truck loaded up with boats and a ton of salt and God knows what else. We got 90 freshies over two nights on the way, and six or seven sharks as well. I don't know what breed they were but they were bad looking buggers.
>
> We went from there to the Nassau where I saw the crocs with the cow. When we got there I had me rifle set, and we went up very slowly to the bank and looked over, and there's this 10-footer looking straight at me. I got right down low and boom! Took the top right off his head!

Plant and Walker waited for the bigger croc to make an appearance, but when he did it was for a brief instant before he submerged again.

> He came up three times, but before I could get that cross on him and squeeze the trigger, he was down again. He knew we were sweating on him and each time he came up for air he showed his snorkel, but not his eyes. Now that's a rare occurrence and you're lucky if you ever see that, because when they put their nose up they've got their eyes up looking for something at the same time. He was smarter than me.

Not to be outdone, Plant and his mate were determined to get their quarry, one way or another.

> We decided to try and net him, using army camouflage nets that Bill Weare came by after the war. He got a truckload of 'em and we still had a heap left. We put them in the water, zigzag fashion, and got out the harpoon, thinking we'll get this bugger this time. We were feeling around on the bottom with the harpoon . . . feeling . . . feeling . . . ah! Here's something! It was part of the hide of the cow we'd seen from the air. They'd eaten most of it and of course the carcass was gone. Well, later on he grabbed the harpoon but quickly let go. They don't like steel!

Plant was fed up and knew he had to resort to tactics that were illegal but part of the experienced bushman's armoury. Dynamite!

> I had a full packet of 8-inch gelignite and I knew how to use it! I'd dynamited dozens of tree stumps on Dad's farm and wasn't scared of the stuff. Anyway, I made up three charges and cut the fuses so they'd all go off together. I gave Cliffy one and I had two and we lit them together with a cigarette. We threw them in and they went whoom! whoom! whoom! and 20 feet of water shot up into the air. Killed every fish in that waterhole, thousands of sleepy cod and bony bream—but not one barra [barramundi]. The crocs would have cleaned them out.

And no crocodile surfaced, dead or alive. Frustrated, the two shooters decided to camp the night and wait for the croc's body to appear—but well away from a low bank the animals obviously used to enter and exit the water.

> We didn't sleep there. Should have, I suppose, but we were both a bit shit scared. We camped 50 yards the other way. Next morning there's this track of fresh mud and flattened grass, and I followed it to the Nassau River, 300 yards away. The track went straight into the river from the top of a 12-foot bank. We never saw that croc again!
>
> You'd reckon the concussion from the dynamite would have killed him, or at least forced him to come up gasping and thrashing about. I would have bet on it. But no, somehow he survived and walked across to the river. An incredible story and another big lesson I learnt. He was the 14- or 15-footer who got away!

Plant's whacky sense of humour extended to other incidents involving the highly dangerous use of dynamite in the company of unsuspecting mates.

> Well, you weren't supposed to use it, so there was a trick I used where I'd light a stick, watch the fuse sputter for a few seconds, and then toss it to whoever was standing next to me and say, 'I'm not going to do it, *you* do it!' Of course he'd shit himself and throw the bloody thing as far away as he could into the water! So I could rightly claim it wasn't my fault, I didn't do it!

Plant says he didn't come across too many other shooters during his time in the Gulf and on the Cape, mainly because the nature of the profession meant living a solitary existence in isolated territory well away from other shooters. Some of the great characters stand out in his memory, though, and he recalls them with his customary sense of humour and a touch of cynicism.

> I didn't have anything to do with the Crocodile Shooters' Club and only met one of them—Lloyd Grigg—once, and that was in front of the Cairns Post Office in 1952. Those fellows with their big hats were a joke as far as we were concerned. Vince Vlasoff had the boat and they shot plenty of crocs, and good luck to them, but we used to have a good laugh about their exploits.
>
> We ran into Jack Vance and Henry Hanush on the Starke River one night. Jack had a six-month beard and a .45 on his hip, and Henry was much the same. Jesus they looked wild! Henry shot a lot of crocs around Princess Charlotte Bay and lived a hard, tough life. He was a good, genuine bloke.

(Henry Hanush shot himself on board his boat, anchored in the Endeavour River off Cooktown, in November 1973. He was 46 years of age.)

Two unidentifiable shooters also rate highly on Plant's list of unforgettable characters.

> Among the toughest shooters I ever saw were a couple of blokes Dad and I, and two or three others, ran into on the Staaten River when we arrived there to shoot in two boats, but these blokes had beaten us to it. They'd also been into the Naussau before us so there wasn't much we could do about that. They were from the Northern Territory and

> were both half-starved and living on sharks. They told us they had been on the grog in Normanton, and left without stocking up on tucker, but we counted 16 croc carcasses on the bank, so they hadn't been mucking around. We gave them one of two big dampers Dad had made, and left them to it. They were about as tough as you can get.

Tough as Bob Plant himself, one of the last living legends of the tough-as-nails lifestyle of crocodile shooting that has long since passed into Australian folklore.

6 JACK SWEENEY

Jack Sweeney, like all his famed crocodile hunter mates, got into the shooting business by chance and through a lust for adventure. But just to make it that far, he had to have a lot of luck on his side to survive five years of living dangerously with the Royal Australian Navy during the Second World War.

Sweeney was born in Atherton, north Queensland, in 1920 and spent his first years moving from town to town with his policeman father. He was following in his father's footsteps as a police cadet in Brisbane when the war broke out in 1939. He joined the navy as a stoker, because 'I failed at everything else!', and spent the war serving on Australian minesweepers and escort corvettes, escaping enemy torpedo attacks and surviving numerous air raids in Singapore, where he and a fellow stoker were cut off from their ship and spent several days 'living like rats' in the ruined city.

'We were more or less living on what we could scrounge and sleeping in burnt-out buildings,' he said. 'We ended up coming across the Dutch army and they gave us a bed in their barracks and some tucker until we found some Aussie sailors from the corvette *Maryborough*, and we joined them doing night patrols to keep the Japanese subs out.'

At war's end, Sweeney was on board the Australian destroyer HMAS *Warramunga*, seconded to the United States Navy, at the signing of the peace treaty with Japan. 'We were anchored half a mile off the *Missouri* when the treaty was signed. The Yanks had 800 planes active that day. They didn't trust the Japanese not to pull something as a last resistance.'

Sweeney left the navy with '900 pounds' in his pocket, a large sum of money in those days, mainly as a result of some entrepreneurial 'wheeling and dealing', including buying a large quantity of watches in South Africa and re-selling them at a handsome profit back home. In 1947, Sweeney rejoined the police force for two years but the yearning for adventure took over when he saw a newspaper advertisement calling for interest in a crocodile-shooting expedition to the Northern Territory. Sweeney was hooked. 'I had to put up 250 quid and off we went, 10 blokes and three vehicles. The problem was, as it turned out, nobody knew what they were doing, and the whole trip was a disaster! We shot a few crocs, but not many—more by good luck than skill!'

Sweeney pulled out of that group and set off in search of adventure on his own. Before long he teamed up with a former British army major and the pair decided to get some money together for some serious croc shooting.

'I went building in Darwin and my Pommie mate got a job droving,' Sweeney said. 'Six weeks later we met up again, pooled our money, and got some shooting gear and a boat together, then headed down to Wyndham. That was another disaster!' Booked into the town's hotel, a local asked to borrow one of their rifles and promptly went off and threatened to shoot his girlfriend with it! Sweeney and his mate found themselves in court and fined 10 pounds each for possessing unregistered firearms. 'We couldn't take a trick at the time. Our boat was too under-powered for the 30-foot tides over there. We were on the beach one night and the tide came in so fast it put the fire out before we could cook our tucker!'

Eventually the intrepid pair managed to shoot a reasonable number of freshwater crocodiles in the Ord River and return to Wyndham with the skins, only to find the skin buyer was the magistrate who had fined them over their rifles!

> We went back to Darwin, picked up our old Jeep and decided to head down to Melbourne. Our luck wasn't so good on that trip either. Between Darwin and Alice Springs we copped 26 punctures. We worked out that hundreds of army trucks that used the road during the war had scattered nails all over the place. We repaired every puncture by hand.

In Melbourne, the two mates booked into the YMCA and that night their vehicle was broken into and all their shooting equipment stolen. That was the final straw and the partnership dissolved.

Sweeney got a job picking peas and beans, earning '28 pounds in 10-shilling notes' before successfully applying for a job at the Woomera rocket range, then under construction, where it was so cold 'I couldn't even roll a cigarette!' He stuck it out for 18 months, saving all his wages, before returning to Brisbane. By chance he met crocodile shooter Lloyd Grigg, who was heading north with Ted Pearce, a young policeman on holidays.

> We met up again in Cairns in 1951 and went shooting for a while on the Russell River and around Mossman. There was hell to pay but we got away with it. Later we loaded up a Land Rover and trailer with our gear and set off for Cape York Peninsula. It took us three days to get to Cooktown, the road was so bad. Further north there were no roads at all in places, just bush tracks, or you followed the scars on the trees, if you could find them!

Sweeney joined Vince Vlasoff on the *Tropic Seas* for the Australian Crocodile Shooters' Club expedition to Princess Charlotte Bay in 1951, but spent most of his time with Lloyd Grigg and Vern Slatter shooting on overland trips.

> Vince showed us the lay of the land, what we were up against, and all the rest of it, then we just went ahead and did it.
>
> We had a half-tame dingo we picked up somewhere, and one night when we were camped near the Cooktown railway station, this dingo cleaned up the stationmaster's three ducks! We weren't too popular for a while!

> We shot all around Cooktown, got 32 salties out of the Endeavour River in a week. The locals never realised how many big crocs were in the river so close to town.

Sweeney has mixed memories about his shooting exploits around the rivers and creeks in the Cooktown area. On the one hand he got plenty of crocs for the lucrative skin industry, but it was also where he nearly lost his life in an encounter that was too close for comfort.

'That was my closest shave to getting cleaned up by a croc,' he recalled.

> I was in a plywood dinghy with a little one and a half horsepower motor borrowed off a local half-caste bloke. He was rowing at the time, up one of those creeks, when I saw a croc with his back out of the water. This was a bit unusual, but I decided to have a shot anyway. Normally you stand up and shoot, but this time I sat down for a better angle. I fired and clipped him on the side of the head, I wasn't quite sure exactly where, but in any case he opened his mouth and came straight for the dinghy, from about 20 feet away. I didn't realise at the time that he had been resting on a rocky ledge . . . I thought he was floating.
>
> Well, he was coming straight at us with his mouth wide open. I had to stand up, eject the shell from the .303 and put another one in. By this time he had his bottom jaw through the bottom of the dinghy and I shot him downwards through the head. If I'd panicked I might have missed him and shot myself in the foot!

It was night-time and I was using a spotlight, so I had to juggle that as well. You imagine holding a spotlight and a rifle, having to reload with a big croc coming at you from 20 feet away! He turned out to be 13 feet, a big lump of a saltie! So anyway, we managed to push the broken ply back in, and we both sat on one side to keep the water out and paddled out of there. We went back the next day, picked him up and skinned him.

My theory is he wasn't going for me but he was going for the shortest possible way to deeper water, and he would have gone right over the top of us. He would definitely have bitten me as he went past!

As Sweeney pointed out, croc shooters 'learned the hard way as we went along' and couldn't afford many mistakes.

Sweeney and most of the early shooters sun-dried their croc skins by hanging them from trees before applying an arsenic-based solution to prevent them getting fly-blown in the humid conditions. 'You always had to make sure you camped where there were big trees along the riverbank. You had to stand on top of your vehicle to nail the 14- to 15-footers high enough to dry out.'

Sweeney, Lloyd Grigg and Vern Slatter spent five months shooting out of a base camp at Laura, where the local policeman managed to combine his official duties with a spot of 'patrol' work in the bush! 'He was a great bushie and after he'd done his paperwork he used to come with us—always on police patrol, of course!'

That five-month shooting spree earned Sweeney enough money to buy an Endeavour River waterfront property near

Cooktown, where he built a shack and 'competed with the flying foxes for mangoes' during the fruiting season. For 16 years Sweeney sold his skins to a Cooktown dealer for the going rate of 'one shilling and threepence an inch for freshies and two shillings and sixpence an inch for salties'.

Sweeney maintained good relations with cattle-station owners on the Cape, but later an influx of amateur shooters, many of them 'new Australians' (European immigrants) spoiled the bond that had been carefully established between the professional shooters and the pastoralists. 'They'd shoot at anything that moved, rarely knew how to use a rifle properly, and mostly ended up getting barred from private land,' Sweeney said.

> We helped the Cape people, who had massive problems with big crocs eating horses and cattle. It was like a smorgasbord for crocs up there. Not only stock, but wild pig, wallabies, turtle, geese—they'd come down to drink and the crocs would knock them off! They had the best menu and apart from a few of us allowed on the land by the owners, those crocs were fairly safe. I'm sure there are crocs up at the heads of those rivers that have been there for a hundred years.

In 1955, Sweeney headed off to greener pastures in New Guinea, where the mighty 1052-kilometre Fly River and its thousands of estuaries and waterways beckoned. It was a hunter's paradise, but daunting and dangerous.

Sweeney bought well-known expatriate shooter George Craig's property on the waterfront at Daru, near the Fly's broad delta where it flows into the Gulf of Papua, and remained there for 13 years. During that time he also teamed up in business with another Australian shooter, Richard Ralph, a partnership that endured for five years.

> In '55 there was no overland shooting because there were no roads and the bush was too thick to get through. You had to have a good boat and know how to run it, and you had to know how to handle the natives. You had to have a good supply of trade goods for them, like knives, batteries, salt and so on, because the money you paid them was worthless unless there were things to buy!

As in Cape York Peninsula, Sweeney's adventures on the Fly River were fraught with danger and narrow escapes from death.

> You made sure you didn't run your boat too close to a high bank, because the crocs sleep on overhanging trees and don't hear the noise of the motor until you're real close, then they panic and jump into the river—they can easily land in your boat! They do that on the Cape, too.
>
> I had one flip just in front of us, flat in the water. If he'd been on a slightly different angle we'd have had serious company in the boat!
>
> Occasionally we'd hear of a native being taken by a croc, but there were plenty we didn't hear about! Same on Cape York.

In 1963, Sweeney travelled to Singapore and bought a '60-foot, 60-ton' cargo boat and, together with a friend 'and a couple of beach bums we picked up', sailed it back to New Guinea. 'You can navigate 520 miles up the Fly and you've got to have a good, strong boat like the one I got in Singapore. As far as I know it's still around, crayfishing out of Thursday Island.'

During a nine-month continuous croc expedition on the Fly River, Sweeney came home with 3000 skins. 'We shot no matter what the weather was doing. We got 110 crocs up to 10 feet in one night, which wasn't bad going.'

With Papua New Guinea's independence in 1975 came a change of attitude towards the Australian shooters, and Sweeney saw the writing on the wall.

> Towards the end Europeans were barred from shooting crocs, so I started buying skins instead and exporting them. The big problem was the natives speared a lot of crocs and ruined the skins, but I still made a lot more money just trading than I did shooting, because I handled a bigger volume. I reckon I handled 60,000 skins and that's a lot of crocodiles!
>
> I had the Fly River to myself for the last five years—no croc shooters or traders apart from me. I was the last of the European shooters and in a way I was sorry to leave. But our time was up and there was nothing we could do about it.

Today, Sweeney alternates between residences in Brisbane and Cairns and still makes souvenirs from crocodile skins bought from farms.

7 RON AND KRYS PAWLOWSKI

Of all the bold and colourful crocodile shooters who lived and hunted on Cape York Peninsula during the middle of the 20th century, there was no husband and wife team as internationally renowned as Ron and Krystina Pawlowski. The Pawlowskis' famed exploits amount to a celebrated story, but they are principally remembered for an event that established the pair firmly in the forefront of Australian crocodile shooting folklore.

In July 1957, Krys, an attractive blonde Polish immigrant then aged 30, killed Australia's biggest known crocodile with a single shot on the banks of the Norman River near the Gulf of Carpentaria town of Normanton. The saltwater crocodile famously measured 28 feet 4 inches, a monster size that was unheard of in Australia and still draws scepticism from some people today.

Nevertheless, the shot made her a worldwide celebrity and earned her the nickname 'One Shot Krys' and a place in the *Guinness Book of Records*. It was the shot that made her a legend. Just below the eye, a sudden and perfect kill.

Yet it was also the shot she later regretted, a split-second in time that took the life of a two-tonne saurian that was almost certainly unique among the tens of thousands of the species that populated northern Australia. 'I would never shoot one like that again,' she later said. 'It was such a magnificent specimen.'

Ron and Krys Pawlowski's arrival in Australia and subsequent journey into Cape York Peninsula's crocodile heartland followed separate yet similar beginnings in the horrors of war-torn Eastern Europe.

When Ron was 13 years old in Poland, his father, a wealthy banker, was shot by the Gestapo in front of his eyes, and his mother imprisoned. The family house was taken over and used as the Gestapo's regional headquarters. Homeless, the young Pawlowski found his way into the Polish Resistance movement, where he became a teenage guerilla and explosives expert, blowing up railway communications and bridges. He was arrested and thrown into a prison camp in Slovakia when he was 18.

Despite the hardships he endured at the hands of the guards, Pawlowski managed to learn English from a fellow prisoner. Desperate for freedom, he escaped by overpowering a guard and made his way to the Allied lines and safety, where he worked as a welfare officer for the Americans. After the war, Pawlowski migrated to Australia by ship, landing in Perth where he worked for a time as a translator in refugee camps.

Krys and her family were also tragic victims of the Second World War. Her schoolteacher father was arrested by the Russians and never seen again. She was taken prisoner with her sister, mother and grandmother and sent to a labour camp in Siberia when she was 13. Two and a half years later they were released in a prisoner exchange deal between the British and the Russians and sent to British East Africa, where she married her first husband and her two sons, Stefan and George, were born.

After her mother and sister moved to England, Krys migrated with her husband to Perth, where her daughter Barbara was born. But the marriage soon fell apart and the resourceful young woman, now with three young children, rented a large house and sublet its rooms in order to feed her family.

By this time, Ron Pawlowski was a gold prospector, kangaroo shooter and skilled bushman who could turn his hand to just about anything to earn a living. Occasionally he travelled to Perth for supplies, usually staying at a hotel for a rare spot of luxury, but on one occasion he had a dog with him and was forced to book into a boarding house—by chance the one managed by a young Polish mother. Ron was captivated by Krys and the Pawlowski crocodile shooting partnership was soon to begin.

George Pawlowski remembers the excitement of leaving Perth with his family—including his new 'dad'—in an FJ Holden loaded up with all their belongings and heading east across the Nullarbor Plain.

'All our possessions were on top of the roof in one of those suction-cup roof racks and when you hit a bump it would all fall off,' he said.

> The Nullarbor was all rough dirt and you mightn't see another car for three or four days. You always carried number eight fencing wire and a soldering iron in case you broke down. Dad could fix anything with that wire, using Coca Cola as soldering flux.
>
> We had no plans for the future, we were just making our way around the country to see what turned up.

The family headed north at Port Augusta and for the next few months took on odd jobs in mining camps and lived off their wits and what the land provided. They made their way to the Top End of Australia through Alice Springs, Tennant Creek, Mount Isa, and on to Karumba, arriving there in September 1955, just as the FJ Holden finally 'conked out'.

The wet season kicked off and the Pawlowski family was stranded. Karumba was a lonely outpost in those days, its only residents the river boat pilot and his offsider, and their families, plus a fisherman, Lloyd Clarke, and a couple of eccentric loners. Clarke, the first professional fisherman in Karumba, is credited with discovering the vast quantities of prawns in the Gulf of Carpentaria—a discovery that led to a 'gold' rush and the multimillion-dollar seafood industry that followed.

Ron built a shack out of bush timber and old iron sheets scavenged from a meatworks that had closed down during the war, and fed his family with fish and whatever he could shoot in the bush, mainly dingoes and feral pigs. Dingoes had a bounty that paid two shillings and sixpence for each skin. Occasionally, to make ends meet, he helped the boat pilot maintain the river channels.

The Pawlowski family got into the 'crocodile business' in 1956 in an unexpected, dramatic way. Ron was busy working on his vehicle 50 metres back from the beach when Stefan ran up, breathlessly shouting, 'Dad, Dad . . . a crocodile . . . Barbara!'

'I looked up and God Almighty, there was my four-year-old daughter Barbara playing on the beach with her back to a 12-foot crocodile,' Pawlowski recalled. 'I reached in the car and pulled out my heavy-calibre rifle and blew the croc's head apart with an expanding bullet.' George Pawlowski described how that incident changed everything.

> An old-timer in the town helped us skin the crocodile. It was a bit of a butchered job, but we sent it off to a dealer in Brisbane and finished up getting 10 quid for it. In those days 13 quid was the basic wage, so Dad thought we were on to something here.

In typical Pawlowski do-it-yourself fashion, the family set to and built a five-metre timber boat out of whatever materials they could scrounge. The bow was cut from an old she-oak tree with a handsaw, second-hand plywood and battens were trucked up from Mareeba, and bits and pieces out of the abandoned meatworks building were all utilised. 'Dad made nails out of thick copper wire and cleaned up old, rusty bolts with tapping dies. Just about everything in that boat was made by hand,' George said.

> Mum and Dad would go out for two weeks at a time in that little boat. They'd wait for calm weather and hug the coastline, shooting crocs until there was only about four inches of freeboard.
>
> The captain of a big cargo ship once told us he couldn't believe we went out in that little boat we called *Joey*. He said it looked like a cork bobbing around!
>
> My sister would be sent off to friends in Mount Isa and my brother and I would stay at home and look after ourselves. Then Steve went to boarding school and I was the original home-alone kid. From the age of about 11 or 12 I used to shoot wallabies for meat, catch my own fish, and survive no trouble at all.

The Pawlowskis 'had no idea what we were doing' when they started shooting crocodiles as a profession. As well as shooting for skins, Ron and Krys captured live crocodiles for overseas zoos and the Australian 'road shows' that were popular in the late 1950s and early '60s. Working at night by spotlight they caught crocodiles up to two metres long by hand, jumping from the boat onto the animal and tying a rope around its jaws.

During one such capture, Ron landed on the crocodile with his genital area 'too close for comfort' to the saurian's jaws, which promptly snapped shut with the usual terrific force.

> I was fortunate he had closed his jaws a fraction of a second before that part of my anatomy—which determines whether I have a squeaky voice or not—came any closer to his teeth. A quarter-inch closer would have been too close. I got

> away with minor skin injuries and the croc got away with my bathers.

On another hair-raising occasion, Ron jumped on the back of a larger crocodile by mistake. It was about '11 foot' and very angry. Struggling in waist-deep mud, Ron yelled out to his son Stefan in the boat: 'Shoot him son, shoot him!'

'But the croc's head was very close to me and we were moving about rapidly so Stefan was too afraid to shoot in case he hit me,' Ron said. 'Luckily I managed to get in the right position to let go of the croc and he took off like a rocket towards the water.'

Stefan and George became expert shooters like their parents and were often out in the wild on their own hunting expeditions. 'My brother Steve and I got a real fright one day when we were out shooting,' recounts George.

> We'd shot a 14-footer up on a bank and Steve had just pulled himself out of the mud and was laying on its back. As I looked across, the bloody croc's eyes were open! He'd been shot but he wasn't dead! I yelled out, 'Steve, be careful mate, the croc's alive!'
>
> Well, Dad always taught us not to make any sudden movements, so here is Steve with his unloaded gun in one hand and his head close to the croc's head. Steve moved forward a bit, very gently, and slowly loaded the gun. Then he very quickly jumped off and put another bullet in him and finished him off!

The Pawlowskis didn't take long to establish themselves as efficient crocodile shooters and for a decade hunted the rivers and waterways of the Gulf and Cape for their prey. It was hot, dirty and dangerous work, but Ron and Krys had survived the terrors of war and held little regard for fear and danger in their adopted land.

The redoubtable Krys soon made a name for herself internationally as the glamorous female shooter who wore jungle green overalls, bright red lipstick and immaculate, painted nails. She made headlines in the London *Sunday Express* as 'The Blonde Who Hunts Crocodiles', and for years featured in numerous news and magazine stories around the world. She became an expert taxidermist after completing a course by correspondence at a university in the United States and soon established a lucrative market for mounted crocodile hatchlings. At home in Karumba busloads of tourists regularly turned up to meet the 'crocodile woman' and buy souvenirs.

She famously told reporters while sipping champagne during a press conference in Brisbane that: 'Even though I spend hours day and night wading thigh deep through mud and swamps, it's good to catch a glint of my nail polish as I pull the trigger of the rifle.' It was a good quote and spread rapidly through the media.

Krys also made her name as a crack shot with both an elephant gun and handgun. Although she'd never handled a firearm before arriving in Karumba, she learned fast from her experienced husband. 'She was better than me with a pistol and she was much better with a rifle at moving targets from a boat,' Ron told enthralled journalists. 'We could both hit a bottle top at 100 yards, but Krys could shoot through the same hole a second time.'

George agrees that 'One Shot' Krys was aptly named. 'Mum was the best shot and she could skin a croc twice as fast as any man,' he said. 'She could beat anybody.'

> There was a shooter they called Harry Whiskers, who was a European like Mum and Dad. He told people there was no woman who could skin a croc faster than he could. Well, they got two nine-footers and they started skinning at the same time. Mum had finished—washed, cleaned and salted the skin—and was already having a smoke when Harry finished!
>
> There was a lot of mythology built up around Mum, like stories of her standing on the verandah of a pub, beer in hand, swearing like a drover. Mum would have a few drinks occasionally, but you'd have to get her in the right mood to talk to reporters. She thought what she did was no big deal, and she never went out looking for publicity.
>
> At first she didn't attract much attention. Most croc shooters were men. Vince Vlasoff took his wife Olive with him, but he did most of the shooting. Mum and Dad did it together, mainly at night-time. Dad used to steer the boat and hold the spotlight, he was good at that, but Mum was a better shot.
>
> We never killed anything we couldn't use. We used to eat crocodile tail, because we observed what nature did. After we'd skin a crocodile we'd watch what the hawks and eagles and crows ate, and it was always the tail and the eyes.

The Pawlowskis taught themselves photojournalism and cinematography and excelled in both. Ron sold close to 300 feature stories around the world and was awarded a certificate of excellence in the 1963 Kodak Photographic Symposium in New York. The following year he won a bronze medal for still photography at the New York World Fair.

One of Ron's seven documentaries, *Woman's Strangest Job*, featured Krys in action, shooting crocodiles in the wild, and was received to great acclaim internationally. 'I went everywhere with a gun in one hand, a camera in the other and a typewriter in my swag,' Ron declared during an interview in the late 1990s.

By 1965, the Pawlowskis had established Australia's first experimental crocodile farm at Karumba on a four-acre block of land leased from the Queensland Government. The family experimented with breeding animals from eggs collected in the wild. They also studied the crocs' feeding habits, including the effects of various types of food on their skin.

It was pioneering work, and Ron and Krys became early conservationists in the field of crocodile preservation. One idea was to donate a certain number of incubated crocodiles to the government's Parks and Wildlife department to be relocated back to the wild. They were convinced that crocodile farms and careful management of resources would preserve the species. 'Crocodile killing had begun to disgust me, as did any other kind of hunting that involved killing,' Ron said.

As a shooter-turned-conservationist, Pawlowski toured Australia and America espousing his cause, lecturing and showing films and slides to appreciative audiences. He addressed the United Nations on his theme of saving crocodiles from extinction, and soon forged an international reputation as a respected authority on the subject.

But when Joh Bjelke-Petersen came to power in Queensland in 1967, the Pawlowskis' call for crocodile protection fell on deaf ears. Legal shooting continued. 'I wanted to ban the export of all crocodile products, which would have resulted in the preservation of the animals, but the political attitude of the day was "if it moves shoot it, and if it grows cut it down".'

Ron said a bitter campaign was waged against his conservationist movement, and he was targeted by a government intent on destroying his business and influence. The special leasehold on his crocodile farm land was revoked after he refused to soften his outspoken public comments against the government. 'The lease was unceremoniously resumed by the government, which had only two years earlier promised in writing to grant us a freehold title,' he said.

According to George Pawlowski, the Bjelke-Petersen regime went to ridiculous lengths to silence his father.

> They even tried to get him on a firearms charge. In the film *Woman's Strangest Job*, Mum is shown shooting a croc with a revolver, and she didn't have a licence for it. As a matter of fact it wasn't hers. Dad borrowed it for the movie. Anyway, a friendly copper tipped Dad off that there was going to be a raid and to get rid of the gun. We were told the order came from the top in the government. It was one of many vicious attempts to shut Dad up by the corrupt government of the day.

In 1968, sump oil was dumped in the Pawlowskis' crocodile pools, endangering the entire stock. Ron and Krys cleaned the animals by hand with detergent and only one died. It was an act of sabotage that bitterly disappointed the couple. In December that year, Ron Pawlowski shot his entire stock of 140 crocodiles, destroyed much of his research material, and walked away from the farm.

But the former crocodile shooter never gave up his determination to protect his one-time prey, and in 1972 he was invited to give evidence to the federal House of Representatives Select Committee on Wildlife Conservation. He told the committee Queensland's crocodile population had declined by 98 per cent since the 1950s and recommended a total ban on hunting the species.

That same year, the federal Labor Government announced a total ban on trading in crocodile products, effectively protecting both saltwater and freshwater species from hunting. As a consequence the Queensland Government placed the crocodile under the Fauna Protection Act. By 1974, Pawlowski had won his battle against a government that ruled what he once called 'Australia's largest wildlife racket state'. 'The result of my defiance is the survival of the crocodiles in the wild, and now burgeoning crocodile farming industry across Australia's tropical north,' he later wrote.

Ron and Krys Pawlowski estimated they shot and killed 10,000 crocodiles—half that number credited to Krys. Legend has it she only missed three times!

In 1998, at home near Mareeba, the woman who shot the world's biggest saltwater crocodile said she was 'really sorry' to have ended his life. 'He never woke up and he never knew we were there,' she said. 'He was the most beautiful animal.'

She said the last crocodile she shot looked at her as if to say, 'Don't shoot me', but she was forced to because he had a bait hook embedded in his body and would have died a slow death in the hot sun. 'I was sorry to shoot them in the end.'

Ron, the fearless crocodile hunter who forged his name as a killer of the species, but later became its greatest protector, agreed. 'If someone offered me a million dollars to shoot a crocodile now I wouldn't,' he said.

Ron still lives in Cairns, happily retired. In March 2004, 'One Shot Krys' Pawlowski died peacefully at home.

8 LOUIE KOMSIC

Crocodile shooters were, out of necessity, a tough breed of men, but one of the toughest of them all was a Yugoslav refugee by the name of Alojz Komsic. After his arrival in Australia from his Communist-dominated homeland in 1961, Alojz soon became the more Aussie-friendly 'Louie', and he went on to join the legendary shooters of Cape York Peninsula.

Komsic became renowned as a fearless hunter who spent months at a time shooting crocodiles alone in the rugged forests and swamplands of the Cape. He was the ultimate bushman, surviving in the harsh terrain using skills learned from Aboriginal elders. He shunned shooting partners, depending instead on his instinctive knowledge of the world around him, and the self-belief that there was no obstacle he couldn't overcome.

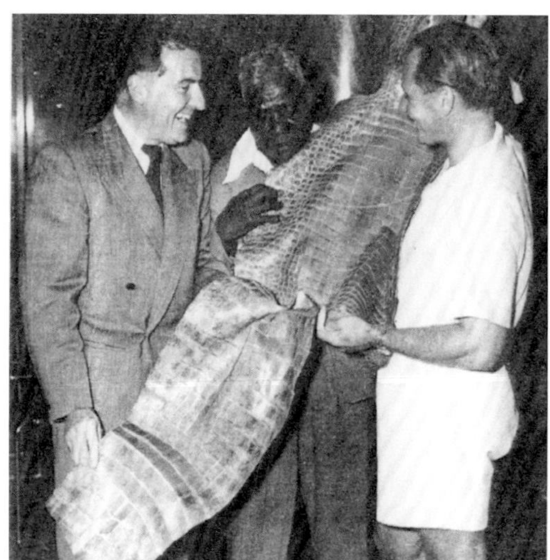

Rene Henri (left) and Vince Vlasoff (right) with guide Toby, inspecting a tanned crocodile skin. [Australian Shooter's Journal / November 1984]

Vince and Olive Vlasoff inspecting a large crocodile skin. [Vince Vlasoff Collection]

Vince Vlasoff dressed to kill. [VINCE VLASOFF COLLECTION]

Bob Plant Snr with Bob Plant Jnr's Uncle 'Aussie' Price and crocodile skins, Atherton Tableand, c. late 1940s. [BOB PLANT]

Australian Crocodile Shooters' Club 1951 expedition: (left to right) Lloyd Grigg, Jack Sweeney, Vern Slatter and John Bergin. [JACK SWEENEY]

Bob Plant in 2007 with crocodile skull. [ROBERT REID]

Lloyd Grigg sizes up the prey in 1953. [Lloyd Grigg]

Jack Sweeney with 13-foot crocodile near Endeavour River in 1951. [Jack Sweeney]

Ron and Krys Pawlowski at Bynoe River, Cape York Peninsula, c. late 1950s. [Ron Pawlowski]

Louie (left pic) and Luba (right pic) Komsic at Cape York, c. 1960s. [Louie Komsic]

Mick Pitman and Fred Nona displaying tanned crocodile hides at Cooktown. [Robert Reid]

George Craig capturing killer 17-foot crocodile on Fly River, New Guinea, c. 1967. [George Craig]

Bryan Peach, age 25 in 1961, with 9-foot freshwater crocodile skin. [Bryan Peach]

George Craig feeding Cassius in 1997. [Robert Reid]

DAILY Sun

BRISBANE, FRIDAY, FEBRUARY 14, 1986
Phone: 253 3333, Classifieds: 253 3111 ★ ★

30c
(Higher in some country areas)

TV: Page 18

They called her Captain Kate

By MALCOLM ANDREWS

THE tough-talking, hard-drinking fishermen who ply the Gulf of Carpentaria called her Captain Kate.

And they treated her just like one of the boys.

That's because Kate McQuarrie, victim of Tuesday's horrific crocodile attack near Karumba, was a bona fide ship's captain — only the second woman in Australia awarded the right to skipper a prawn trawler.

"It's hard to prove yourself in the fishing industry — doubly hard if you are a woman," she told me two years ago, just after she'd passed the exam for her A1 master's ticket.

That ticket meant she could skipper craft up to 50m long.

On holiday at Ballina, NSW, two years ago, Kate explained that in January and February it wasn't worth a fisherman's trouble to go prawning.

Barramundi

"The catch is dismal. You're scratching to cover fuel, let alone pay for your tucker," she said.

Ironically, this year she didn't take a holiday but turned her hand to fishing inland for barramundi.

Fishing had her hooked.

"It's all I want to do for the rest of my life," she told me. "I love it."

The love affair began six years ago, when a boyfriend talked her into signing up with him as cook on a trawler.

"I had heard awful stories about what a cook was expected to do," she recalled.

● Cont Page 2

Croc victim Kate McQuarrie — one of only two women entitled to skipper trawlers — in the wheelhouse.

'A short but deadly swim'—newspaper report about Kate McQuarrie's death.
[Daily Sun / February 14, 1986]

Cassey Bond (right), victim of Jardine River crocodile attack, with his family.
[The Cairns Post]

Komsic was a professional crocodile shooter from just after he arrived in 1961 until shooting was declared illegal in 1974. Apart from a stint in the Northern Territory, where he also shot wild buffalo, Cape York Peninsula was always his favoured stamping ground. By his count, he shot around 40,000 crocodiles of all sizes on the Cape.

Like many young men from post-war Europe, Komsic came to Australia in search of freedom and new frontiers. He was one of 16 children in a family active in the Resistance during the war, and although none of his family was killed by the occupying Nazis, some were forced to serve in the German army.

Komsic said he was a 'larrikin kid' who quickly learned to use his wits to stay alive during and after the war when 'there were bombs and land mines laying around and exploding everywhere'. Later, the young Komsic was conscripted into the Yugoslav army for two years. After that he escaped Communist rule and made his way to a refugee camp in Italy run by the United Nations. He hoped to migrate to Brazil and 'chase the diamonds', but changed his mind when shown a film about Australia and its wide open spaces, including a section on crocodile hunting.

His first home in his new country was an Italian immigrant camp near Melbourne, but the enterprising newcomer was soon out working in factories until he saved enough money to head north towards the crocodile country he had heard so much about. Komsic spoke very little English, but he knew how to work hard, and a few weeks cane cutting in Tully, north Queensland, got him the stake he needed to set himself up as a crocodile shooter. He was a stranger in a strange land, but he knew how to 'give it a go' in true Aussie style, and he was soon respected for it. 'I liked the true-blue pioneering blokes that were around in the '60s,' Komsic said, still speaking at age 72 in the thick accent of his Bosnia–Croatian heritage.

> I liked those men and I said to myself 'I'm going to learn that attitude', so I watched the ringers in the pubs, drinking and fighting, and the one who falls down buys the beer.
>
> I had a few fights. I shouted the first bloke who knocked me down, that was in the Normanton pub. From that day on I was good mates with every bastard, because I had the guts to have a go, and I was accepted as a good bloke.

Komsic adopted the outback Australian way of life as though he had been born into it. Like the other professional shooters, he learned how to hunt and skin crocodiles by trial and error, and lived rough in the scrub.

But Louie Komsic did it all his way, shooting at night with a spotlight, alone in a dinghy deep in the heartland of crocodile territory, where one mistake could mean a horrible death. He liked to get close, very close, before firing at his target.

> When you go shooting crocodiles at night, you don't have to be a crack shot, because you don't shoot from far away, but get in close with a high-powered rifle and kill him instantly.

> I'd sometimes shoot in the daytime, but then I'd use a telescopic sight if I saw a croc across the river. You've got to be a good shot doing it that way.
>
> To be honest I don't believe a crocodile shooter who says he never missed. I shot one and hit him in the wrong place and he nearly killed me. I hit his nerves and he went mad, rolling and thrashing about in a narrow creek with steep banks. He smashed my dinghy and I lost my rifle. I had to get out of the water and walk up the creek to my camp. The next morning I went back with another rifle. The big croc was there, just looking at me, so I shot him.

At the peak of the crocodile-shooting era in the 1960s, when skin prices were at their highest, the best of the shooters made a lot of money in a relatively short time and thousands of crocodiles were killed to meet the demand. Komsic's best haul was 36 saltwater crocodiles, averaging two to three metres, in a single night. Up to 20 a night was common. Freshwater crocodiles are smaller, easier to kill and skin, so the numbers shot were higher.

Just after arriving in Cairns in the early 1960s, Komsic met 15-year-old Luba Senius, a German-born daughter of Ukrainian immigrants.

> Louie rented a room above a café owned by my friend's parents and that's how I first met him. I was still going to school then. We started going out together when I finished school. Mum and Dad didn't like it much, because he was so much older, but we got married in 1964, and they gradually got used to the idea.

Although Luba travelled with her adventurer husband on crocodile-shooting expeditions, mostly he preferred to be alone—just him, the bush and his prey. On one occasion the police knocked on Luba's door and informed her that her husband's Toyota four-wheel-drive vehicle had not been picked up as arranged and he was missing, presumed dead. But Komsic had been cut off from his vehicle by floodwaters and was camped in the bush, shooting crocodiles and totally unaware that he was the subject of an extensive search. 'I saw planes flying up and down at one stage, so I put out my fire and hid in the scrub,' he said. 'I didn't want to confuse them because I thought they might be looking for somebody who was lost, but I didn't know they were looking for me!'

One month later, Komsic emerged from the swamp and went home, wondering what all the fuss was about. 'I always knew he'd be all right, because he'd been away for months at a time before, but things can happen,' Luba said.

Komsic has twice travelled solo down the vast Mitchell River from Mount Carbine in the east to the Gulf of Carpentaria in the west, a 500-kilometre journey across almost the entire breadth of Cape York Peninsula. The Mitchell's catchment area covers 72,000 square kilometres of tropical rainforest, eucalypt woodlands, large areas of wetlands, plus treacherous marshes and mangroves. The river and its numerous tributaries harbour not only crocodiles, but giant gropers and bull sharks. It is a remote, dangerous area, where even a minor injury can spell disaster.

But such things didn't worry Komsic. On the first trip, he shot and skinned 960 freshwater crocodiles in nine weeks, salting and storing them along the way in carefully prepared pits dug into the earth and covered with logs and hessian bags. The skins were picked up on subsequent forays along the river system. 'The Mitchell has the most freshwater crocodiles because it's such a huge river,' he said. 'But I also got 750 skins in three weeks on the Lynd River.'

Komsic has had his share of near-misses on the wild rivers of the Cape.

> A couple of times I've lost my supply boat and everything in it, guns, batteries, all my food, going through rough water. I learned that you always have a spare gun, bullets and batteries safe in a watertight drum, so it will float and you can always find it later. You've got to have a gun to survive, but there's plenty of food—crocodiles, pigs, birds and fish. I lived for one and a half months just off the land.

Komsic has a special affinity with Aboriginal people and, from his earliest days shooting crocodiles, he learned first-hand the ancient techniques the Aborigines used to survive in their harsh land. He makes fire the way they do, and follows their traditional bushcraft skills as closely as he can.

> I never asked questions but watched what the old men did. If you can start a fire, you'll never be cold or hungry. I learned that you never wait until you're hungry before you hunt. If you do you'll get nothing, because you're impatient to eat and you've got no brains. You make sure you have something to eat the next day before you get hungry.

Komsic occasionally met up with his fellow shooters and took time out to 'have a drink' and relax from the serious business of crocodile hunting.

> We'd get two or three gallons of rum, no shooting, but just go drink at a camp somewhere on the river. Not much talk, just drink. Cook damper to eat. I'd bring a few cartons of beer, you can't keep rum up all the time, but I'd always hide one bottle of rum, because some of those blokes can be stroppy bastards if you run out. If we get low we mix rum and port, and when we finish grog we go back to work.

In his 14 years shooting on the Cape, Komsic worked every major river 'two or three times a year' and each time he left them, the rivers were quiet, as though they were 'shot out'. 'When I left a river you would swear there are no crocs left, but they're hiding. You shoot what you can shoot, and the rest are hiding. As soon as they see the light, they're gone, but they were there.'

Komsic says he can 'smell' a crocodile downwind for 'half a mile', especially if the animal has just eaten a meal.

> They burp and I can smell them. It's a particular smell, and if you don't know that test of smell you might think there's no crocodiles in that particular river, but when they breathe out I know they're there.
>
> The worst thing is when somebody is eaten, then everybody jumps on the river and starts shooting innocent crocodiles, but a crocodile with a body in him, doesn't

> matter what body, a man or a kangaroo, that croc will disappear and make sure he's in a safe place.
>
> I've told the police if they want me to find a crocodile that's eaten somebody, don't let anyone there until I come and I'll find him. He has to burp and I will smell him. You learn that over the years.

Komsic believes that fatal crocodile attacks on humans are nearly all the result of mistakes made by the victims.

> Very rarely is a person killed when he's doing the right thing. Generally people get on the grog and start yahooing. The worst thing you can do is go on the river and yahoo, splash the water. If you do that, the nearest crocodile is going to come and have a look.

Komsic ventured to New Guinea for a brief shooting trip on the Fly River, where he met fellow shooters George Craig and Tom Cole, but he soon returned to familiar territory on Cape York. 'I spent about a month up there but the natives were spearing crocodiles and they'd come on your boat. Too many problems.'

But as more and more weekend shooters with modern vehicles and equipment flooded into Cape York, shooting undersized crocodiles for trophies, or just target practice, Komsic began to have second thoughts about his profession.

> There was indiscriminate killing of very small freshwater crocodiles and for a number of years I wrote to politicians to try and stop it but they weren't interested and didn't bother replying.

I'd see heaps and heaps of little carcasses under three feet around the creeks and rivers, and I tried to stop it, but nobody would listen.

One day I decided to stop. I'd caught a small crocodile and was about to put a screwdriver through his eye to kill him for stuffing later on. He looked at me and I couldn't do it. When I came home I said to Luba, 'I don't want to do this no more, if you don't mind,' and she says, 'I hate what we're doing,' so we put the chemicals away and never killed another one after that.

It was time for new challenges. Komsic switched from shooting crocodiles to professional fishing, specialising in catching the internationally prized barramundi from his base on the shores of Princess Charlotte Bay.

Even fishing has its dangers and on one occasion on the Normanby River a sawfish thrashed its way out of a net on to the boat's deck and mutilated Komsic's left hand, almost severing his thumb in the process. Only the prompt intervention of the Flying Doctor, and a fast flight to Cairns, saved his thumb.

In 1974, Komsic purchased a 30-year special lease for Marina Plains cattle station, a spectacularly beautiful property fronting Princess Charlotte Bay. Komsic had long-term plans for the 7000-hectare station. His dream was to build a homestead for his family and construct a multi-purpose tourist and maritime facility on the waterfront.

There was just one unforeseen problem. Marina Plains was bordered on three sides by Lakefield National Park and the state government wanted to resume the land and include it in the park. 'I saw a wonderful opportunity there for my son and grandson and a place where people could come and stay and enjoy the environment,' he said. 'I felt like a king there, and I knew I could achieve something important for the future.' But the then National Party Government had other ideas and so began a long battle for Komsic to hold onto his land.

> I didn't mind it becoming a national park. All I asked from the government was to let me have one square kilometre of land for the homestead and other buildings, and four kilometres of Annie River frontage for fishing and tourist boats. But they came and took the property off us anyway.

Komsic rejected several offers of $50,000 from the government, but was finally forced to accept the cheque, which went towards paying his legal bills. 'When the Labor Government came into power they took the land off us, and that was that.'

Louie and Luba Komsic managed to battle on with their Palmer River Goldfields Roadhouse, a whistle-stop restaurant and bar for truckies and station hands on the Peninsula Development Road south of Laura. The roadhouse was little more than a shack when the Komsics purchased it in 1979, but with typical shoulder-to-the-wheel hard work and perseverance, they built it up into a popular tourist drawcard on the road north. The family sold out after nearly a quarter of a century and moved south to Cairns.

But adventure was never far from Louie Komsic's mind, and he wasn't finished with the outdoor life in his beloved

Cape York wilderness. In 2007, at the age of 72, the one-time refugee 'new Australian' was back full-time professional fishing, chasing barramundi in the pristine rivers that flow into Princess Charlotte Bay. 'I don't want to sit around and be a burden to the government and my children,' he said. 'I've got a boat, and if there's fish out there I can catch 'em.'

Louie Komsic, the quintessential loner, packed up his gear and was gone.

9 GERMAN JACK AND CROCODILE MICK

It was a strange partnership, but one that was not out of place in the frontier lifestyle of Cape York Peninsula in the 1980s. They were crocodile hunters in an era when the practice had been banned by law, but that didn't stop the maverick pair of bushmen from flouting the rules. 'German' Jack Kiel and 'Crocodile' Mick Pitman were deliberate poachers of the protected species, modern-day outlaw hunters who made and lived by their own rules.

They were known as 'river rats' around the waterways of the bauxite-mining town of Weipa, on the far north-west coast of the Cape. Tough and fearless, and with little respect for authority, Kiel and Pitman made an illegal living from crocodiles, curing and expertly manufacturing skin products and selling them on the black market.

They hunted outside the law for 10 years. Kiel was the

teacher, the master shooter. Pitman was his protégé, the willing student who followed in his footsteps.

But it all ended on 25 May 1990, when Jack Kiel was brutally speared and bashed to death in the Stubby Hut, a favourite drinking spot for Weipa regulars, at the mouth of the Embley River on the town's waterfront. Kiel's body was found after hours crumpled on the floor of the pub's deserted open area by a local truckie. The croc shooter had suffered 32 stab wounds to his face and body from a fishing spear, and his skull had been crushed. An autopsy later revealed he had died from a punctured heart.

A local man, Warren Anthony Smith, 23, was charged with the murder and remanded in custody. The vicious killing had allegedly occurred as a result of a dispute over two cartons of beer, but the case ultimately failed due to insufficient evidence. It was a tragic end to the life of the enigmatic German. He was 57 years of age.

Hans Gerhard Kiel migrated from Germany in the 1950s and set himself up as a plumber in the Northern Territory. However, he was soon lured by the promise of big money into shooting freshwater crocodiles for a living. From there, after a stint working on the Snowy Mountains hydroelectricity project, he moved to Cape York Peninsula, where he found a lucrative market existed for the larger saltwater species.

In 1967, after shooting around Cape York from his base at Weipa, Kiel ventured north to New Guinea, where he met up with G.J. Craig. Kiel was with Craig on a four-week hunting trip on the Fly River when they captured the famous crocodile nicknamed Oscar, a beast that measured 'between 17 and 18 feet'.

Craig remembers Kiel with respect and admiration for his skills.

> I first met German Jack on Jack Sweeney's boat on Thursday Island when we went across to Daru. He turned out to be a very good hunter, very reliable, and a good man to back you up.
>
> Jack liked the life of a croc hunter, roughing it for two or three months at a time in the swamps and mangroves. He always preferred to catch the big crocs alive, rather than shoot them, and we took a lot of risks together to do that.
>
> He was a terrific bloke, but aggressive when he got drunk. In those early days he didn't drink as much as later on, when he went back to Weipa. He became a big drinker, but not a good drinker.

After his adventures with Craig in New Guinea, Kiel returned to his old camping area at Weipa. At the end of 1979, just before the start of the monsoon season on Cape York, Kiel met up with a young Tasmanian who was working as a contract plumber for Comalco, the giant bauxite-mining company. Mick Pitman tells the story of his first meeting with the notorious German.

> I was walking back from the Stubby Hut with a carton of beer over my shoulder when I was approached by a stocky, grubby, bent-nosed bloke, who bummed a six-pack of beer

off me. I didn't know who it was at first, until a friend told me it was German Jack.

I really wanted to get into the croc hunting game and later on when I ran into him again I bailed him up and said, 'What about a trip up the river for that six-pack you owe me?' He wasn't keen, but finally said, 'Okay, get a drum of fuel, a dozen beers and a bottle of vodka and meet me on Friday night.'

Pitman's first trip 'up the river' with Kiel was an initiation into crocodile hunting that turned into a nightmare when the German ordered him to put down his rifle and jump into the water on top of a croc, telling the frightened novice the animal 'was only a six-footer'. 'Well, I did it because I wanted to impress the German, but I was shitting myself,' Pitman recalled. After Pitman had been rolling and 'near drowning' in the muddy water with the juvenile crocodile for a minute or so, the laughing German told him to stand up. The would-be hunter had been wrestling the crocodile in barely knee-deep water and didn't know it! 'That was the start of the best 10 years of my life. Ten years of solid adrenalin-pumping action with the real Crocodile Dundee!' Pitman said.

Pitman was born in Launceston and spent his early years out in the hills 'shooting rabbits and anything you could eat'. After serving a plumber's apprenticeship he found his way to Cairns to work for a ship-building company constructing navy patrol boats.

But it was the boozing, brawling Barbary Coast strip of waterfront pubs that was the main attraction. 'They were the days of the hotels, the nightlife, the women,' he said. 'It was wild, and I loved it.'

Pitman was soon looking for more action, though, and, after answering an advertisement for plumbers in Weipa, set his sights on the biggest adventure of all—crocodile hunting. The German Jack and Crocodile Mick poaching team was about to form.

'Crocodile shooting had been banned for a few years before I arrived but that hadn't worried the German,' Pitman said.

> He had no time for scientists or authorities—he just kept on shooting 'the geckoes' as he called crocs. He didn't miss a beat.
>
> He wasn't tall, but he was as strong as a bull. His nose was all over his face from fighting, and he had fingers like sausages. The soles on his feet were as thick as leather. I've seen him stand on red-hot embers while he was welding and he wouldn't feel a thing.

Kiel was never seen dressed in anything but his cut-down jeans shorts, a blue singlet and his trademark black beanie. He lived alone—but was often visited by other 'river rats'—in a tin humpy on Roberts Creek, at the mouth of the Hey River, a few minutes by dinghy from Weipa.

Pitman was given permission by the Wik Aboriginal people to live on their land at Tranjam Point, about eight kilometres from Kiel's camp. Together, the two men poached crocodiles under the collective nose of the authorities—but not without attracting official attention. Pitman said he had been 'raided' 26 times by various wildlife authorities, but was only charged once—escaping a penalty by telling the magistrate he was 'only after fish to feed my family'. Although during their early years together, Kiel and Pitman shot crocodiles to make their leather products, they later switched to capturing them alive for taxidermy purposes.

Pitman said the biggest croc he ever captured was five metres in length, caught using a harpoon attached to a float by a long rope, which eventually tired the animal until it could be captured alive.

> We made all sorts of things from the skins—handbags, shoes, even condom pouches—and stuffed the smaller crocs, which we caught by hand. We sold them in the pubs and on the ore ships that pulled in for bauxite. Tourists loved our hand-crafted products.
>
> We never raped and pillaged the environment. We only caught the ones we could use, and left plenty in the wild to breed. We weren't vandals. And most people didn't want us to get busted. We were tolerated and protected in a way. We even had some friends in the Parks and Wildlife department who used to look the other way, and the Aboriginal community loved us because we'd remove the problem crocs that were giving their women and kids a worry.
>
> The German used to say, 'A still tongue is a wise one. Keep your mouth shut and nothing will happen.' He was pretty bloody right, too!

Pitman lays claim to shooting, harpooning and manually catching a staggering 16,000 crocodiles of all sizes during his

10-year illegal spree with Kiel. He said the two men once caught 70 of the animals in 'an hour and three-quarters'.

'I learned everything off the German. He was my mentor and father figure and he was the real deal. German Jack was the first and only Crocodile Dundee, never mind the movie bullshit.' Kiel certainly played the Dundee part with flair. In 1987, he described a dangerous crocodile encounter in a magazine interview.

> We were out on a wooden pontoon in pitch darkness when we harpooned a 14 foot croc. It was a bad shot, landing just above the croc's tail where all the nerve endings are. It went into a death spin and rolled so fast the harpoon smacked one of the other blokes in the head and knocked him out.
>
> I was pulling on the harpoon line when it suddenly went slack. Next thing I know, the croc has smashed up through the floor of the pontoon. Again it went into a death spin, then disappeared, leaving the water pouring into the vessel. Luckily we got to shore before it sank. We killed the croc the next night.

In his last years Kiel became a serious drinker. Pitman said he carried the German out of the Stubby Hut in a fireman's lift many times when he was dead drunk. 'He was a hard drinker who would go on a week or two's binge, but then you would see him running and pushing weights to keep fit. He was hard to figure out, but a great bloke.'

Pitman said Kiel was a gifted musician, who played guitar like a professional.

> He was simply amazing. He'd play left or right hand, drunk or sober. Jazz, rock'n'roll, flamenco—you name it, the German could play it. His singing left a lot to be desired, though. His favourite party trick was to grunt like a croc while he was playing.
>
> He was pretty secretive about his life in Germany but I think he was classically trained. Apparently his father was a jazz musician during the war.

Pitman said the news of Kiel's death left him reeling with shock and grief.

> I hadn't seen him around for a couple of days because I'd been out in the bush. When I went to town I saw his dinghy tied up on the bank at the Stubby Hut and reckoned I'd have a couple of beers with the German. I walked in but couldn't see him and the local blokes were very quiet. Then they told me what had happened.

Pitman looked at where the police had outlined a body on the floor and walked out of the pub.

> I kept to myself for a few days. I felt like a piece of me had gone. I made myself go to his camp and collect his photos and papers, like he wanted me to. Somebody had been there, the place was wrecked. His stuff was well hidden, and I was the only one who knew where the photos and documents were. He always told me never to sell his photographs, and I never will.

Pitman and Kiel's close friends built a concrete memorial at the slain crocodile hunter's campsite. His hut was demolished. 'We always thought a croc would get the German because he had a habit of sleeping outside by the river,' Pitman said. 'We never thought he'd go this way.'

In 1996, the Queensland Environmental Protection Agency declared an amnesty for all hunters who had been operating illegally. Mick Pitman took the opportunity to 'come out of the bush and into the paddock' and become a legal crocodile skin craftsman and taxidermist. Pitman is a leading advocate for the introduction of legal safari crocodile hunting expeditions.

10 BRYAN PEACH

Bryan Peach, like all his fellow crocodile shooters, headed for Cape York seeking adventure. The family farm on the banks of the Murray River in Victoria held little appeal for his restless nature. He'd heard about buffalo and crocodile hunting in the north of Australia and the urge to have a go was irresistible.

Peach learned to handle a rifle as a boy in the swamplands bordering the farm. Ammunition was scarce so he had to shoot straight and make every bullet count. That turned out to be good training for his later career as a crocodile shooter.

In June 1959, at 23 years of age, he packed up his utility and, with a 100 pounds in his pocket, drove up the east coast of Australia to Cairns. There he met local hotelier Paul Kamsler, who was also a crocodile skin buyer, and Peach was quickly off the mark and heading bush.

But 'making a quid' proved to be slow progress and the novice shooter took a while to learn the ropes. Eventually he teamed up with an Aboriginal 'tin scratcher' named Freddy Thomas who, as a miner, knew the Lynd and Tate river systems west of Chillagoe like the back of his hand, and off they went to try their luck. 'I learned the trade from scratch,' Peach said.

> It took us two hours to skin our first crocodile, a six-foot freshie. A crocodile's skin and flesh are one, not like a warm-blooded animal where you can just pull the skin off, like a rabbit or a kangaroo. You have to cut a crocodile's skin off, like skinning a fish fillet.

That year Peach and Thomas managed to shoot enough crocodiles to pay their expenses, but it became clear that Peach's utility would not handle the muddy bush conditions of the approaching wet season. The two men decided to cut sugar cane for a few weeks, an enterprise Peach called 'the worst job I have ever had, or hopefully, ever likely to have'.

At the end of 1959, Peach drove home to help his father harvest crops, and while he was there borrowed enough money to buy a used Land Rover and equipment for his second foray into crocodile country. Soon he was a true professional shooter, but with a difference from the other shooters of the time. Peach hunted mostly from land, and he concentrated on the freshwater crocodile for a very good reason.

> Saltwater crocs paid the best, three dollars an inch in those days, compared to one dollar an inch for a freshie, but you

could shoot 10 times as many freshwater crocs as you could salties. It was a matter of volume equals more money.

It was also less risky with the freshies, you were in fresh water and there were fewer problems with flies and mud, and life was generally more comfortable. I always reckoned you shot salties for glory and freshies for money.

The big crocs were a pain in the arse. The skins can be half an inch thick and take a bag of salt to preserve just one. Very often they're not a first-grade skin, they've got scars and been knocked about, and you've got to skin them in the water so you can turn them over. The best size is about three metres, which will give you 20 to 22 inches of skin, nearly always first grade, which was worth in today's terms 1000 or 1500 bucks.

I shot the salties when I saw them, because they'll come 100 miles up the rivers to the big lagoons, where there's plenty of fish and game, and they'll make a place for themselves.

Like all shooters, Peach couldn't resist the lure of the *big* saltie when the opportunity presented itself.

We were in Burketown one night and we were told there was a big croc downstream from the Nicholson River crossing at Escott Station. They reckoned it was about six metres long so we decided to go out and shoot this bastard.

We had an aluminium 10-foot boat and we paddled down to a fork in the river where we saw this big bright eye with probably half a dozen freshwater crocodiles around it. We paddled quietly closer. I never liked aluminium boats, they drum too much, it's not a natural sound, but we managed to get pretty close.

It was a big croc. I reckon the eyes were eight inches apart . . . six inches apart would mean a 15- or 16-footer. We were fairly close to its head, about 30 feet or so, and at this point a bloody trevally jumps into the boat with a hell of a noise! Well, we nearly shit ourselves! We were a bunch of nerves and I had the shakes—you get highly strung with a big crocodile probably five feet longer than the boat you're in. Well, the croc disappeared, but at least we got a fish for breakfast!

Freshwater crocodiles are not man-eaters, but they can bite and do plenty of damage, as Peach can attest. 'I shot a small one and climbed down the bank to grab it by the nose. It twisted in my grasp and I had to let it go, but I got my hand ripped for my trouble. You had to be careful, freshie or not.'

Even for an experienced shooter, nature often played illusory tricks in the harsh and dangerous environment of Cape York. Peach was once idly gazing at a group of about 30 logs on the far side of a lagoon when one of the 'logs' got up and entered the water, followed by the others. Subsequently, he shot more than 100 freshwater crocodiles in two weeks. The following year, during a long drought, the lagoon dried up completely.

Peach said his preference for solo hunting was risky, and at times monotonous, but it had its rewards. 'One of the strangest things about the bush is the eerie silence. Out there on your own you're almost afraid to break the silence, that it would be sacrilege to shatter the mood created by the stillness. It was very strange.'

Peach's choice of firearm for shooting freshwater crocodiles up to two metres was a BSA single shot .22 rifle, a gift from his father on his fourteenth birthday. Crocodiles over two metres needed more serious attention, such as the army .303, which was cheap to buy and used readily available ammunition. He used this firearm to shoot an unusually big 'nine foot six' freshie on the Flinders River—one of three that size he shot during his career.

Peach finished his crocodile shooting career a year before the shooting ban came into effect in the early 1970s. By that time there were far fewer crocodiles than there were in the 1950s and '60s and most of the crocodile shooters had retired or moved on to other ventures.

'We made big money back in the 1960s,' Peach said. 'You could make enough money in two months to buy a house. It was hard but it was lucrative if you were serious about it, but there were only a few of us who were serious hunters.'

PART 2: FATAL ENCOUNTERS

11 PETER REIMERS: EATEN ALIVE

Weipa is a small town on the north-west coast of Cape York Peninsula, about 830 kilometres by road from Cairns. It's a company town that was owned and run by Comalco, but bought by RioTinto in 2000, and is situated on the world's largest bauxite deposit. The town was established in the early 1960s by a special act of Queensland Parliament, which handed control to Comalco. It's a remote outpost, isolated from the south by flooding rains during the summer wet season. Weipa is also a fisherman's paradise, where a smorgasbord of reef and river fish abound in numbers unknown in the more populated regions of north Queensland. There is hunting too, with feral pigs a favourite among local recreational shooters. There is also a healthy population of saltwater crocodiles, grown large and bold by an absence of human predators since protection was introduced.

Weipa has been the scene of numerous 'frontier' incidents over the years, including wild alcohol-driven brawls and violent deaths, accidental and otherwise. Back in the 1970s, it was a place that largely ignored society's rules, shunned outsiders, and jealously looked after its own in troubled times. Nothing much shocked or disturbed the hardened souls who chose to live and work in Weipa.

Nothing much, that is, until the horrific events of Friday, 25 April 1975. On that Anzac Day holiday, Comalco plant operator Peter Reimers, 32, set off with two workmates on a shooting and fishing weekend to the Mission River, 45 kilometres east of Weipa.

There was nothing about this trip the three men hadn't done before. Reimers and his mates, Doug Goeldner and Bob Kirby, headed into the bush looking forward to a haul of barramundi and mangrove jack and a few beers around the campfire. But this was destined to be no ordinary weekend of fun and mateship. Instead, it was to become the weekend from hell.

When they arrived at their camping spot, Goeldner and Kirby launched a dinghy to try their luck for an early catch in the river. Reimers, however, set off in his Land Rover for a spot of pig shooting, yelling out to his mates: 'Keep me a mangrove jack!' Apparently, Reimers was not fond of barramundi. Those few light-hearted words were the last Goeldner and Kirby heard from their mate.

Writing about that fateful day years later, Goeldner described what happened next.

> After getting some barra and jacks we came back to camp. Finding no sign of Peter being back from shooting yet, we decided to go look at the swamp we knew he was going to. Finding his Landrover, we fired several shots in case he was in hearing range but no reply. Being just on dark we went back to camp, hoping he might just be lost and hopeful he might return during the night.

But he didn't, and the two friends spent a long night in growing apprehension for the safety of Reimers.

At daybreak they headed back to the swamp, but Reimers was nowhere to be seen. After inspecting Reimers' vehicle and scouring the immediate area, Goeldner and Kirby steeled themselves for a wider search, telling themselves they'd find Reimers on his way back to his vehicle. Goeldner continues the story:

> From there we walked across to a small fresh water creek. Walking up the creek for two kilometres finding nothing, we turned and back tracked to where we first hit the creek. We then proceeded down the creek for a few hundred metres. On rounding a bend in the creek, we came across Pete's clothes and watch. They lay at the base of a tea tree with Peter's rifle leaning up against it on the very edge of the bank. At this spot a well-beaten cattle pad was visible. It being a shallow crossing just downstream from a weedy, grassy narrow deep hole. On observing the crossing of knee deep water, we could see Peter's boot marks where he had walked down into the shallow water to cool off. From there could be seen six boot marks spread a long way apart

> where he had run down the bed of the creek. Then we spotted one boot mark, one metre up the bank and claw marks each side where he had been chased and caught as he tried to leap up the bank to get his rifle. The croc had to drag Peter's body back through shallow water to get back to the narrow deep hole before he could have drowned him. This would have been all in the space of a few minutes.

These are chilling words from Goeldner as he recalled the terrible discovery of Reimers' boot marks and the mind-numbing realisation of what had happened to his friend.

Goeldner and Kirby drove back to Weipa to notify the local police sergeant, who at first thought he was being set up by an elaborate joke. It was late afternoon when the party arrived back at the site of the tragedy, and in the fading light, police photographed the scene and Reimers' clothes and rifle.

The next day, Sunday, a convoy of vehicles arrived at the scene. Searchers, including trackers from the Weipa South Aboriginal community, split up into two parties, one heading upstream and the other downstream. Goeldner described what happened next.

> Roughly where Peter was taken I saw one leg floating on the surface near the bank. I pulled it out and a few minutes later the police yelled out they had found his other leg a bit further downstream. A further search upstream by Bob and myself, and we spotted one of Peter's shoes snagged on a tree branch on the surface. At the same moment a large croc head surfaced and spotting us let out a great snort and slowly submerged leaving behind a ghastly rotten smell.

The discovery of their friend's remains was a nightmare experience for the searchers, especially Goeldner and Kirby, still struggling to accept his bizarre fate.

A mining engineer and explosives expert in the search party used two charges of gelignite to blast the hole where the crocodile disappeared, but there was no immediate sign of the animal. The party then blocked the downstream exit to the hole to prevent the crocodile floating past with the current. A 'tinnie' was launched and after a fruitless hour gaffing submerged logs, the crocodile's carcass was finally hauled to the surface. The size of the rogue crocodile has been reported as large as '19 foot' but the search party put the beast's true measurement at just under five metres. Goeldner says:

> We towed the croc with a 4WD out onto the bank. It was 16 foot long and it was a real old fighter as he had one large front tooth missing, plus his back right leg. Also a few feet of tail, but none of this had slowed his attacking ability too much. At this stage the croc was opened up and the rest of his body was found inside, mostly intact.

Peter Reimers was a well-liked member of the Weipa community. He was an experienced bushman and was well aware of the dangers inherent in the waterways of Cape York Peninsula. How such a practical and bush-savvy hunter could be attacked and eaten in a small creek remains a mystery. Whatever the circumstances were that caused Reimers to let his guard down in such dangerous territory, he paid the ultimate price for his mistake—a death so gruesome that the mind almost rejects the reality of what must have taken place before he finally succumbed to the ultimate horror.

12 BERYL WRUCK: DEATH ON THE DAINTREE

Daintree township, 140 kilometres north of Cairns, 21 December 1985. It's nearly 11.30 on a hot, humid Saturday night. The town broods silently on a bank, high above the starkly beautiful Daintree River. The wet season is late in tropical Queensland, and there's a mood of oppressive expectancy in the still, sultry air. Soon it will rain every day, torrential downpours as regular as clockwork. But right now the energy-sapping heat is getting people down. It's a bad time of the year, when tempers fray, and it doesn't pay to look too hard at your neighbour.

But just down the dirt road, three kilometres around the bend leading into town, there's a pre-Christmas barbeque in full swing at Michael and Jackie Turner's Butterfly Farm. In a setting of lush rainforest and sweet-scented blossoms, a small party of Daintree residents eat, drink and dance into the night. Right on 11.30, four of the revellers detach themselves from the main group, and wander down a boardwalk to the Turners' private jetty, on the edge of Barratt Creek. It's almost low tide, and the creek is flat and lazy, imperceptibly moving downstream to its junction with the Daintree River.

The four sit and chat awhile, occasionally stopping to listen to the myriad insect sounds tumbling from the eerie darkness along the water's edge. A single hurricane lamp hangs from a post, casting dim, flickering shapes across the creek. Somebody suggests a dip to cool off. The four move out on to the jetty, and stare down at the brackish water.

Maurice Mealing has lived in Daintree all his life, but has never been to this spot. He doesn't like the look of it. Nevertheless, he strips off his outer clothes and leaps off the jetty. His wife, Sarina, hangs back. Mealing swims a few strokes in a splashing semi-circle, and climbs back on to the jetty. 'Don't go in,' he warns the others.

John Robb, a burly, bearded riverboat operator, ignores the warning. He takes his clothes off and enters the water. He stays in close to the jetty post, where the water is about a metre deep. He waits there as 43-year-old Beryl Wruck removes her dress and, clad in bra and panties, sits down on the edge of the jetty. He watches as she lowers her body over the side and squats down, turns around to face the creek, and looks sideways in his direction.

Maurice Mealing forbids Sarina to enter the water. She stands behind him watching the others. Off to Beryl Wruck's right, out of range of the hurricane lamp, a patch of rotting leaves and debris floats on the almost-still waters of the creek.

Cottonwood branches hang low, forming a coal-black tunnel parallel to the bank.

In the middle of that patch of leaves, low down, barely above the surface of the water, a pair of ruby eyes glowed faintly. A pair of nostrils sensed the air. A pair of ears listened. The crocodile knew this place well. He had been here before. He was perfectly balanced in his environment. It was his place, and he was master of his own territory. Camouflaged, with timeless patience, he waited.

John Robb, about to get out, with his eyes on Beryl Wruck, lingers a few seconds more in the water. Maurice Mealing has his eyes on Beryl, too. He is watching her when the crocodile makes his move. Beryl is saying something to Robb when the creek explodes in a terrifying rush of power. The huge beast has Beryl Wruck across the hips. Struck dumb with terror, she throws up her arms in the face of death. The crocodile slices the bank with his tail, slewing his body in a shower of mud and water as he lunges for the creek's deep mid-channel. In another split-second of heart-stopping madness, Beryl Wruck is dragged underwater, never to be seen again.

John Robb is left dazed, hanging on to the post. All he saw was a wall of turbulence which swallowed Beryl and knocked him off-balance. From up on the jetty, Maurice Mealing shouts, 'A bloody croc's got Beryl!' Sarina cries out, 'Beryl! Beryl!' Still in the water, shaken, Robb stares hard at the spot where Beryl had been. He wonders what the hell the Mealings are saying. It is less than a minute since Maurice Mealing first entered the water.

By daybreak, David Martin, Beryl Wruck's common-law husband, had scoured Barratt Creek down to its junction with the Daintree River. So had the police, several National Parks and Wildlife Service officers, and a fair percentage of Daintree's male population. One 3.5-metre crocodile had been shot and killed, two more had been hit but escaped, and plenty more, real and imaginary, shot at wildly in a night of bedlam and anger.

When the media arrived, emotions and confusion were still running high. Daintree and the search for Beryl Wruck became instant international headlines. 'Killer Croc' prose flowed freely from the fast-moving pens of a dozen reporters. Camera crews trailed cables over the Butterfly Farm, the Barratt Creek jetty, and through the town.

Daintree River and its tributaries were searched relentlessly. Traps and snares were set, banks and mudflats probed. Crocodiles were shot, and their 'stomachs examined' for human remains. Anonymous shooters killed them in traps set by National Parks rangers, and left them to rot. As expected, it was open season on anything that moved in the river. 'Daintree Folk Want Croc Blood' declared a Brisbane headline. Locals denied the charge, insisting that only large adult crocodiles were being hunted. They claimed that trigger-happy outsiders were responsible for most of the shootings, and had no right to be there. It was David Martin's moral right, they said, to hunt the killer of his loved companion.

It soon became obvious that the situation was out of hand. Bullocks and pigs were slaughtered for bait, gunshots echoed each night across the river, and grim-faced men with spotlights and telescopic-sighted rifles stalked the muddy banks of Daintree's creeks and streams.

By Christmas Day, few crocodiles were to be seen. The fast-learning crocodiles were keeping clear of their predators and old Daintree hands were saying you wouldn't be seeing many crocs around there from then on. The official search for Beryl Wruck was terminated at 5 pm on 27 December, with still no sign of a body. But on that same day, police found two strips of meat floating in Barratt Creek. A subsequent pathologist's report stated, 'The material is fat of animal origin, consistent with human omentum from an obese person, but absolute identification of tissue as being of human origin is not possible.' Beryl Wruck had not been an obese person, and the material was considered unlikely to be part of her remains.

Although the police and National Parks searchers had withdrawn from the river, David Martin was officially sanctioned to continue the search operation. With him was charter boat operator Richard Ralph, a former crocodile hunter with 20 years' experience shooting and trapping the animals across northern Australia and in Papua New Guinea. Ralph was relieved when the search scaled down. 'There were too many idiots on the river,' he said. 'Too many amateurs who didn't know a thing about crocs.'

Ralph and his partner Lindy Brooks were close friends of Beryl Wruck and David Martin. On the night she died the couple were on their boat sailing the Great Barrier Reef when the news came in. 'Lindy bolted out of the cabin and screamed: "Beryl's been taken by a croc!" We turned around straight away and headed back to Cairns. We were in shock.'

Martin had his own plan, and had no intention of quitting the river until he had Beryl Wruck's killer. Late one night, near the Daintree wharf, Ralph shot and killed a crocodile 'over the 3.5-metre mark'. Although he didn't think it was big enough to be the one that took Wruck, Ralph had David Martin in the boat and made a quick decision. 'I couldn't take the chance of letting it go,' he said. 'It was close to town, and David's blood was up, so I killed it.' The crocodile's stomach revealed nothing.

After the first rush of media activity had died down, and the townspeople had reflected on what one described as 'a welter of misquotes, lies and make-believe', they closed ranks and firmly shut down on outsiders. Strangers asking questions were not welcome. Even at the best of times, visitors and newcomers were considered 'others' by hardcore Daintree locals. There's a saying up that way that it takes locals 10 years to forgive you for coming.

Standing in the middle of Daintree's one main street and small cluster of shops, a stranger could sense a difference, a subtle scalp-crawling sensation of *be careful, go easy* in the feel of the town. There was a touch of Alabama in the air, as beer-bellied men in four-wheel-drive vehicles made out they didn't see you, or else they nailed you with mean, warning stares. In many ways, Daintree—crouched on the edge of the vast Cape York Peninsula wilderness—was still a pioneer town, and its 100-odd residents made their own rules.

David Martin's general store was the focal point for the town's trade and social life. You'd step back three or four decades when you entered its dim corrugated iron and timber interior. You could post a letter at the store, or make a phone call from the public telephone outside, if it happened to be working. Although it wasn't a pub, the general store sold stubbies of beer, which you could drink out the back with the locals, if you were game enough, in a rough-and-ready beer garden. As long as you kept your mouth shut, you were reasonably safe.

A group of half a dozen men in work clothes looked up as this writer walked around the corner at the back of the store, beer in hand. I was in Daintree on assignment for a national magazine. The story intrigued me and I had purposefully allowed some time to lapse before journeying to the town.

The men were talking crocodiles, just like everybody else in north Queensland. 'We'll bide our time,' said one, ignoring me. 'We'll wait 'til the cooler months, when they're out sunning on the banks, and then we'll get 'em.'

I had been advised by more than one person to approach David Martin with caution. It sounded like good advice. Martin was a born-and-bred Daintree bushie, a thick-set loner who was used to doing things his own way. People said that he'd changed since he met Beryl Wruck about three years earlier, that he'd mellowed, smiled a lot more. Beryl, on the mend from a broken marriage, was looking for company. She had two grown daughters with families of their own, and a young son who depended on her. When she moved in with Martin, she helped him run the store. Business picked up after that. Beryl Wruck was a fun lady and everybody liked her.

Martin shook my hand reluctantly and without warmth when I introduced myself. It was 17 days after Beryl had died. Martin looked haggard, still in shock. Unshaven and tight-lipped, he told me what I already knew, that he was at the barbeque, sitting on the Turners' verandah, when the alarm was raised. The numerous press statements didn't come from him, he said, and he had nothing more to say to anybody. 'Southerners aren't very popular around here,' he informed me. 'They come up here and try to tell us how to run things. When we're ready in this town, we'll talk about it.' The message was clear and straightforward. I thanked him, and left him to his own thoughts.

John Robb wasn't talking either. I waited at the Daintree wharf until the last tourist had filed off his safari river boat *Kingfisher*. I showed him my card. He wasn't impressed. He told me plainly that Beryl Wruck's death was no business of anybody else's outside the town, and accused me of exploiting the tragedy.

But Robb did speak to me several weeks later concerning media reports that it had been his idea to go down to Barratt Creek on the night of the tragedy. He denied he made the suggestion, saying it would have been out of character for him to have done so.

Daintree at that time was no great place for reporters. One businesswoman, who told me crocodiles are only good for turning into leather, reckoned another night in the town would make me very unpopular. But the desire to impart information is a basic human trait. Sooner or later, people like to unload. Don't use my name, they will say, but this is what happened . . .

Daintree had been a divided town ever since the potential for tourism attracted enterprising newcomers. Michael and Jackie Turner established the first river cruise operation, the Crocodile Express. Later, they sold out to develop a new concept in tourism, the Butterfly Farm. Others soon arrived, bringing money and ideas, and with them an increasing number of day-tripping tourists. But to many Daintree stalwarts, the newcomers represented an intrusion on their way of life. However, before Beryl Wruck's death, the two factions managed to exist together under a shaky white flag of truce.

Crocodiles in the Daintree River had been a contentious issue simmering between locals and tourist operators for some time. Fishermen had warned repeatedly that the crocodile population had increased dramatically since legal shooting stopped in the early 1970s. This was hotly denied by the tourist operators, conservationists, and some independent observers. Estimates ranged from no more than 10 large adult crocodiles in the river, to well over 100. Claims of a 'population explosion' were becoming commonplace, together with demands for a culling program to be implemented.

Andrew Lloyd, together with his mother Billie, had purchased and operated the Crocodile Express, and conducted twice-daily tours of the river. The most crocodiles he had observed on a single trip was eight, including all sizes down to the very young. 'And that was in winter, when the crocodiles were out on the banks and highly visible,' he explained.

Walter Starke, an American marine biologist who had lived on the river in his research vessel since 1979, estimated an average of 10 to 12 crocodiles would be visible on a

12-kilometre stretch of river on a winter's morning. Like Lloyd, he stressed that the estimate included all sizes. 'There *has* been an increase in numbers since I came here,' said Starke, 'but I wouldn't call it a population explosion. More like a stable increase toward a maximum river population.'

It had often been claimed that crocodiles were being fed from tourist cruise vessels on the Daintree River. Nothing wrong with that, said the locals, but some day there's going to be trouble. Certain crocodiles were being treated as pets, earning themselves affectionate nicknames, such as Old Faithful, Chad Morgan and Big Jim. A 'five-footer' called Yo-Yo was a regular visitor to the downriver vehicle ferry crossing. The crocs were getting too familiar with human habits and behaviour. In the old days, according to local folklore, shooting kept the 'cheeky' crocs down, and the remainder gave humans a wide berth. Now they did everything but get in the boat.

Not only were crocodiles being handfed on the Daintree, but persistent reports supported local rumours that the same thing had been happening around the Barratt Creek jetty. It was there that tourists disembarked from cruise boats to inspect the Butterfly Farm. Chilling stuff, even before the night of 21 December.

Public controversy raged over the question of whether Beryl Wruck was in fact the victim of a crocodile attack at all. Only one person was said to have seen 'what could have been part of a crocodile'. That person was not named by police. Maurice and Sarina Mealing's names were never published—they remained out of the media spotlight throughout the drama. John Robb gave his version of events, and stuck to his story—he didn't see a crocodile.

Theories, counter-theories and opinions dominated conversations in hotel bars and living rooms across Queensland and sprang from the pages of newspapers all over Australia. One persistent question was, if a crocodile was indeed responsible for Beryl Wruck's disappearance, why hadn't it employed the famous 'death roll' to drown its victim, as crocodiles are reputed to do with large prey?

Louie Komsic knows more about crocodile behaviour than most people. He points out that the so-called death roll can occur *under* water, or may not be necessary at all—that a crocodile can snatch its victim and keep going in one deadly pass. 'I've seen crocs carrying 50-kilogram pigs, alive and squealing, through mangrove swamps, and I've seen them drag large bullocks off river banks,' he says. Komsic stresses that crocodiles are opportunistic feeders, and unpredictable.

Another theory was that a whaler shark, known locally as a 'bull' shark, could have taken Wruck. Whalers, feared worldwide as man-eaters, have been sighted in the Daintree, presumably to feed and—so popular knowledge goes—to rid their bodies of ocean parasites.

Richard Ralph scoffs at the suggestion that this was how Wruck died. The attack took place at nearly low tide, and a shark big enough to take a human whole will only move upriver on a high tide, he points out. As the tide receded, the shark will move with it back out to sea.

Ralph also had a few things to say on the suddenness and silence of Wruck's death. 'Very few people have any idea how powerful a crocodile's jaws are,' he said.

> You can hold their jaws together with a shoelace—they have very little strength to open up—but on the down-bite it's like two trucks coming together. If that croc took Beryl around the middle and shattered her spine, all the guts would have been driven up into her lungs, and all air would have been expelled in an instant. There would be no breath left to make a single sound.

There was also a hint of foul play. It was rumoured that Beryl Wruck was a prosecution witness in an upcoming murder trial, concerning the November shotgunning execution of suspected drug dealer Frederick Cox at Upper Daintree. But Sergeant Kevin Turner of Mossman Police, who coordinated the search for Wruck's body, denied any possible link. 'Mrs Wruck was not in fact a witness in that case,' he said. 'Her son was, but only in an incidental, very minor way—most certainly not the shooting itself.'

Turner had no doubts about Beryl Wruck's death. He had the policeman's trump card. Two of them in fact. Witnesses Maurice and Sarina Mealing. Although Turner chided the media for promoting 'mystery and drama' into a straightforward case, he conceded a point: 'Yes it is a strange tale. It is.'

Why would four rational people, all of whom lived in the area, go swimming on a dark, sultry night in known crocodile waters? Especially, as Richard Ralph pointed out, when 'The crocs are cranky at this time of the year. It's hot, and they've used up a lot of energy during mating. They're hungry, and on the move. You couldn't pick a worse time to go swimming.' Ralph's comment was logical and based on experience. Nobody swims in or near crocodile territory. Especially in summer, and especially not locals.

Wrong. It was common knowledge in Daintree that swimming from the Barratt Creek jetty often took place. Michael Turner admitted that he and Jackie swam there. Not only that, he said, but they sometimes saw crocodiles near the jetty, 'but not big ones'. *Not big ones?* Local legend suggested that 'fair-sized' crocodiles had been sighted around the banks of the jetty, and even up higher on the Turners' lawn! Two people, husband and wife, said they had been swimming off the jetty the same day as the tragedy, and that it wasn't unusual for others to do likewise. 'I'll never know why we did it—I can't explain it,' said the woman.

Maurice Mealing said he and Sarina never knew about the swimming, nor the feeding of crocodiles at the jetty. 'But it was a bloody stupid thing to do,' he said.

On the other hand, Alec Lyall, an Aboriginal resident of Daintree who had lived in the area all his life, had this to say: 'I wouldn't swim in that river for anything. I was a shooter up on the Peninsula, and I know a bit about crocodiles, enough to leave them alone. That river's got me scared, and it takes a good whip to frighten me.'

How great a part did alcohol play in the tragedy? After all, the barbeque had been in progress since 8 pm, and Daintree folk are not renowned as teetotallers. Maurice Mealing: 'We'd had two or three stubbies each, I suppose. Nowhere near drunk—I can drink a dozen stubbies, no worries, and still know what I'm doing.'

Sergeant Kevin Turner:

> When I arrived, none were in a state of intoxication. I was told they had all taken liquor, but they were just in a party mood. Of course, shock would be a sobering factor, but in my opinion they were in control of their mental and physical faculties. Those people acted completely out of character, and made an unwise decision.

In the aftermath of Beryl Wruck's death, the gulf between tourist operators and long-time locals widened. As the two factions grew further apart, open hostility became rife in the town. Anonymous, threatening phone calls were made in the night, people refused to speak to each other, and a brawl broke out in the beer garden of Martin's General Store. A siege mentality engulfed the town but, although fear and mistrust prevailed, business in Daintree boomed. Tourists flocked to the town, river cruise boats were packed to capacity, and David Martin's store became the subject of a thousand photographs. A Sydney couple on a sightseeing trip narrowly escaped death when their rented Mini-Moke plunged off a bridge into Barratt Creek. But behind the flow of dollars, the tension grew.

On Thursday, 16 January, a 1500-word letter from David Martin was published in *The Cairns Post.* Entitled 'A Few Thoughts from a Citizen of Daintree', the letter stated its purpose was to 'clarify some of the hysterical information which has been bandied about lately'. In the text, Martin accused tourist operators, and the 'conservationists they manipulate' of feeding and protecting the crocodile that killed Beryl Wruck, and of disrupting the search by patrolling the river and 'frightening every croc they saw, making it impossible for the guilty croc to be shot'. Summing up, Martin wrote: 'Can you justify yourselves? How will you live with yourselves when the next person is killed? You already have blood on your hands. You are as bad as the croc we are hunting.'

The day before that letter appeared, David Martin and Richard Ralph caught a five-metre crocodile on a baited line, two kilometres upstream from the Barratt Creek junction. Inside the crocodile's stomach were what appeared to be human remains, consisting of forearm bones, and either finger or toe nails. The next day a Brisbane newspaper quoted Health Minister Brian Austin as saying that tests revealed that the bones were consistent with that of being from a female body. Several weeks later, a Health Department spokesman stated that the bones were those of a white female, but 'it was impossible to prove if they belonged to Mrs Wruck'.

'I doubt that those bones belonged to Beryl,' said Richard Ralph at the time. 'I think there is another croc around, maybe a six-metre one, which either killed her, or shared her remains.' Ralph reconstructed a grim scenario of the attack:

> The croc could have taken her at top speed, possibly 10–15 knots, and shot downstream to a 10-metre hole near the junction with the Daintree. In deep water, with plenty of room, he would have dismembered her with a kind of

whip-cracking motion. Crocodiles can't swallow an adult human whole, and they're small feeders anyway, so they have to break up the carcass. Other crocs would recognise the splashing, and come in to scavenge. I'm certain the croc responsible has taken somebody before.

Beryl Wruck's death created an immediate furore in Queensland politics. Martin Tenni, the Cairns-based Minister for the Environment in the conservative Coalition Government, had been vocal for a number of years on the need to 'shoot out' crocodiles in north Queensland but had softened his stance recently, under pressure from conservationist groups and the tourism lobby. Now Tenni claimed his original stand had been vindicated and called for the immediate removal of 'all known crocodiles' from the Daintree River region. He further announced his intention to propose in State Parliament that private contractors be allowed to tender for the right to remove crocodiles from the natural environment and set up breeding farms for a future skin and meat industry.

Tenni was an outspoken politician, and one who was either loved or hated. His electoral office window had been shotgunned, heavily graffitied, and stoned several times. He claimed this activity was the work of drug pushers and 'Labor Party hooligans'. His public statements were legendary as prime examples of right-wing extremism, but he consistently won votes for the National Party-dominated government. Pressed to define 'all known crocodiles', Tenni replied: 'By that I mean *all* crocodiles, from the day they come out of the egg until they're fully grown. I want my electorate to be a crocodile-free zone.' He went on to comment that, although he deplored the indiscriminate shooting of the animals on the Daintree River, he 'wouldn't want to be the one to tell those people up there to stop, otherwise I might get a bullet myself'.

Tenni's plan outraged conservationists, animal welfare groups, and just about everybody else, but he was determined to stand his ground. 'I'm not going to back off this time,' he announced. 'I'll fight, and I'll fight it all the way, and the greenies and environmentalists can all go to billy-o.'

In a recent interview, Richard Ralph said the passage of time had not altered his opinion that the animal that killed his friend Beryl Wruck is still alive and quite possibly still in the Daintree River.

> There's something suspicious about all this. The arm bone found in the croc we caught was too small to have been Beryl's. Lindy is slightly built and we measured the bone against her own arm. It was shorter, and Beryl was bigger than her, more my stature, so it's not possible that the bone belonged to Beryl. Lindy also said the fingernails found were the wrong shape to have been Beryl's.

Ralph said he and David Martin 'went hell west and crooked' up and down the Daintree searching for the killer croc. Ralph also searched underwater, near the spot they had caught the crocodile with the human remains, using a knotted rope to orientate himself in the murky depths. He found a rib bone that was later identified as female, but it had never been in a crocodile's stomach. 'It was not even partly digested and was covered in green slime. I went backwards and forwards on the rope knot by knot looking for bits the croc would have spewed up when the hook went down his gullet, but I didn't find anything more.'

Ralph admitted that, while he was concerned about live crocodiles and bull sharks during his daring underwater search, he was more worried about the danger from above. 'I was more worried about David with the .308 rifle up in the bloody dinghy, so I said to him: "For Christ's sake be careful what you're shooting at, I don't want to get my head blown off!"' Ralph was 'willing to believe Beryl was taken by a croc', but there was no physical evidence of her death to confirm it.

> We caught two 16-footers and one had remains in it and the other didn't. The remains weren't Beryl's, so whose were they, and where's Beryl? Officially, it was nice and clean, because they don't like mysteries, but a big question mark still exists as far as I'm concerned.

Along the waters of the Daintree River, the memory of Beryl Wruck will haunt the minds of those who knew her for a long time to come. 'We are all guilty,' a Daintree resident said. 'We should have known better. The crocodile is not at fault, because the river is his environment, and he has got to eat.'

13 KATE MCQUARRIE: A SHORT BUT DEADLY SWIM

On 11 February 1986, just seven weeks after Beryl Wruck disappeared into the muddy depths of Daintree's Barratt Creek, another grim tragedy was played out in the isolated waters of Vanrook Creek, a tributary of the Staaten River on the west coast of Cape York Peninsula. It was here, at about 2.45 pm, that 31-year-old Catherine Anne McQuarrie took her last swim.

The deckhand, and skipper Bob McNeil, had been checking barramundi nets when the outboard motor on their dinghy broke down, three kilometres downstream from their anchored fishing vessel, *Kiama*. They walked back along the mangrove-tangled creek bank to a spot closest to the boat and entered the water. On board, fisherman Des Trimble watched as the two started swimming. McNeil reached the boat first. As he turned to assist McQuarrie, barely three metres away, a crocodile lunged and took her. In a few heartbeats, the young woman, known affectionately as Kate, was dead. Like Beryl Wruck, she never uttered a sound. It was Barratt Creek all over again.

The next day Trimble and McNeil sighted the mutilated body of their friend enmeshed in a fishing net, strung out from the boat to the creek bank. Horrified, they watched as a crocodile they estimated to be 5.5 metres in length tugged at the body. Trimble fired a round of high-powered bullets at the crocodile. It rolled and vanished. McQuarrie's body was recovered from the water later that day, when a police party arrived by boat from the prawn fishing town of Karumba, 130 kilometres to the south. The crocodile was not found.

One week after her body was recovered an autopsy revealed she had died from the effects of crushed ribs puncturing and collapsing a lung. The government medical officer, Dr John Corcoran, who carried out the post-mortem examination in Mount Isa, said the victim did not drown. 'With a collapsed lung, Miss McQuarrie would have been unable to breathe. She died quickly after the initial attack. She would have been dead before she went down a second time. The imprint of the massive jaws which dealt the crushing blow was clearly visible on her torso.'

Why did McNeil and McQuarrie enter the water that day knowing large crocodiles inhabited every creek and river in the region?

'There's just no way you could get me to swim in these rivers,' McQuarrie was heard to say after Beryl Wruck died. But it was only a short swim to the *Kiama*, late afternoon was approaching, and neither McQuarrie nor McNeil relished the thought of spending an uncomfortable night in the mosquito-infested mangroves. So they gambled with their lives, and Kate McQuarrie lost. It was a dilemma everyone in the fishing industry understood. On the one hand you never go in those waters; on the other hand you have to get back to the boat.

Privately, several experienced fishermen admitted they, too, would have attempted the swim. 'You'd risk that distance,' one said. 'You'd be thinking about the crocs, but you wouldn't want to camp in the mangroves either.'

Kate McQuarrie was a country girl, originally from Eungella, outside Murwillumbah in northern New South Wales. She was everybody's friend, an attractive, happy-go-lucky type in the male-dominated world of trawler fishing. She was a regular patron of the old waterfront pubs of Cairns—the then infamous precinct that was affectionately known as the Barbary Coast. They called her Captain Kate, due to the fact she held a mariner's ticket in her own right—then a rare accomplishment for a female in Australia. Kate was an old hand in the Gulf waters and coastlands of Cape York. She had skippered prawn trawlers in the Gulf, and her dream was to own her own boat. Fishing was her life, all she wanted to do. She knew about sharks, drownings and other mishaps at sea—and crocodiles. Like her companions in the fishing fraternity, she accepted nature's terms as part of the job, and the risks that went with it.

Bill Ennis, chairman of the Gulf Savannah Tourist Organisation, was also aware of the risk. In a newspaper interview, he said he hoped 'the emotional response' to the attack would not result in the removal of crocodiles from the river systems because of an 'error of judgement' by McQuarrie.

> The lady took her chances. I hope that people do not get this out of perspective. People in the gulf are fully aware of the dangers posed by the crocodile population. However, we have learned to live with them and respect their ways. The gulf is a wilderness area where taking chances is a way of life.

'It is a very unfortunate situation, and the fishing industry will be concerned over the loss of one of its crew,' Ennis continued. 'However, crocodiles and the gulf go together, and to maintain this balance, crocodiles have to be viewed as an occupational hazard in remote and wilderness areas.'

Not so, said the government of the day. Premier of Queensland Sir Joh Bjelke-Petersen went public to reinforce his view that there was an urgent need to eradicate crocodiles from the north. 'Sure they are good from a tourist point of view, but we can't allow this to go on,' he said.

Outspoken advocate for the removal of 'all known crocodiles' from his electorate of Barron River, north of Cairns, Martin Tenni, whose portfolio had by then changed to Minister for Water Resources and Maritime Services, pressed ahead for his agenda with renewed vigour. He said that unlike some conservationists, he considered human lives to be more important than the welfare of crocodiles.

Fishermen weren't happy with living with crocodiles

either, and made it plain that an increase in numbers since shooting was banned had put their lives further in jeopardy. The Queensland Commercial Fishermen's Organisation Gulf area councillor, Warwick Crossland, said McQuarrie's death had reinforced fears within the industry. 'Crocodiles used to disappear when they heard the sound of a boat, but they don't anymore,' he said.

> A lot of people on the boats have children with them. They used to be able to get off and walk along the banks, but now they can't even get off and most of the fishermen carry guns. We live here and contrary to claims by some people, we have not learned to live with them. Fishermen are a different breed, and although they may not say much, we protect ourselves.

Kate McQuarrie had no protection when she entered the dangerous waters of Vanrook Creek on that tragic day, and she paid for it with her life. She became one more name on the list of fatal crocodile attacks on Cape York Peninsula, and a reminder that, in the natural environment of this primeval and savage predator, there is no second chance available to the unwary.

14 CASSEY BOND: THE RIVER OF DOOM

It was to be a joyful 1993 Christmas reunion for the Bond family at the township of Bamaga near the northern tip of Cape York Peninsula. On Christmas Eve, Cassey Bond, 48, his wife Mary and 17-year-old daughter Karen travelled from the nearby Aboriginal community of New Mapoon to meet relatives—who had driven the best part of 1000 kilometres from Cairns in two vehicles for the festive celebration—at the Jardine River ferry crossing. The party included Cassey's brother Horace, his wife Joy (Mary's sister) and the couple's daughter Debbie, all from Cairns, and niece Kerry from Edmonton.

The ferry managed to get one vehicle across the river before it broke down on the second crossing—a not uncommon occurrence for the then notoriously poorly maintained vessel. Cassey volunteered to drive to Bamaga for spare parts. In his absence, Horace and the ferry operator had restarted the engine, but it promptly stalled again.

When he returned, Cassey Bond decided to swim out to the ferry to help the two men. He had lived in the area all his life and swum the Jardine many times during his childhood and youth, as well as the times when he worked as a Telecom linesman. He was aware the river, although relatively shallow at that point—barely two metres at its deepest—was inhabited by crocodiles. He was also aware it was the monsoon, or wet, season, when the animals are aggressive and territorial during their mating period. But he reasoned the noise from the ferry and human activity would keep the crocs at a safe distance. This was conventional wisdom, but seriously flawed with deadly consequences.

It was just before dark when he entered the water. Watched by his wife and daughter on the bank, he struck out for the disabled vessel. He didn't make it. Mid-river, in a flurry of turbulence, he was gone.

Horace Bond's daughter, Debbie, and his niece, Kerry, standing on the deck of the ferry, had seen a 'large ripple' which at first they thought was the trail of a wild duck following their Uncle Cassey. Then they realised it was 'coming too fast'.

Cassey Bond had time to scream 'Help me!' to his horrified relatives before he disappeared under the water. Horace rushed out onto the deck and shouted at Cassey's wife and daughter on the bank not to go into the river. There was nothing anyone could do.

In shock, the family watched as Bond's lifeless body surfaced a few minutes later. They saw another crocodile circling nearby. Almost two hours later, police and volunteers found his body in shallow water barely three metres from where he was attacked. There were eight large bite marks on his torso, but no limbs were missing.

It was a tragic and barely believable coincidence for the Bond family. In June 1980, Mary Bond's father, Ken Savo, was taken by a crocodile in the same river while swimming alongside a dinghy. Like Cassey had been, he was a Telecom linesman and was on his way home from a seminar with several other workers when the crocodile struck. Witnesses said he disappeared without a sound, resurfaced briefly, and then went under again, before anybody could assist him.

Joy Bond said her sister Mary was traumatised by the loss of her husband 13 years after her father was killed in the same way. 'It's very hard to accept that this could happen all over again,' Joy told reporters. 'When I lost my father, it was something I could not get over, and I would not go near the Jardine River.'

And there was also another known fatal attack in the area. Sergeant Trevor Crawford, officer in charge of Bamaga police, said a man had been taken by a crocodile while sleeping on a beach at Umagico, a settlement just outside Bamaga. The man was Cornwall Mooka, 36, a Torres Strait Islander who was last seen stepping from a dinghy and walking towards Cowal Creek, about five kilometres from Bamaga, on 26 June 1987.

On Friday, 3 July, a human ankle and foot were found inside a 3.5-metre crocodile shot by wildlife rangers near a camping area close to Umagico Beach. Several days earlier, human leg bones and Mooka's clothing were found on the beach. The rest of his remains were never located. Forensic tests later confirmed all the bones recovered were those of the missing man.

Many rumours exist of other fatal attacks in the Jardine area, including a report that during the Second World War a soldier was taken at an army camp by a '14-foot monster' while fishing on the banks of the river. Other reports claim an unknown number of Aboriginal people disappeared in the area up to the 1960s, and were presumed to have been killed and eaten by crocodiles.

Sergeant Crawford said the Jardine River had always been notorious for crocodiles and many dogs had been taken in recent years. He warned that an increase in the crocodile population meant logically that the threat to humans had also increased.

Six days after Cassey Bond died, the killer crocodile was captured in a trap by police and wildlife officers at the Jardine River crossing. The 2.8-metre female animal was smaller than expected, but positively identified as the killer by comparing its teeth—some were missing—to bite marks on Bond's body. Originally, it was believed a five-metre animal was responsible for the attack. However, the Bond family remained unconvinced that the captured crocodile was the one responsible for Cassey's death.

Cassey's brother Michael said although he was relieved that a crocodile had been caught, the family was certain they had seen two of them move towards his brother immediately before the attack, and he called on the Department of Environment and Heritage to make the crossing safer by keeping numbers down. 'There should be more done in terms of reducing the population around there, because people still want to use the river,' he said.

Ferry operator Mac Blarrey said two crocodiles had been in the vicinity of the crossing since the attack and he believed one or both could have been involved in the tragedy and could kill again. He said a wildlife officer who was part of the team that trapped the 2.8-metre crocodile couldn't guarantee it was the killer croc. 'I asked him if he could tell me for sure it was the right croc, and he said he couldn't,' Blarrey said. 'It doesn't help me if the ferry breaks down in the middle and I've got to jump for it and swim. I've got eight kids and I don't want to orphan them.'

Local communities in the area weren't too happy about the situation either. In January, a dog was taken on a stretch of beach at Seisia, an Aboriginal community six kilometres north of Bamaga. There were two problem crocodiles in the area that were known to lurk near a camping ground and boat ramp near the wharf. Locals said the crocodiles had taken several dogs and were getting bolder.

Council chairman Joseph Elu said he'd had enough and was prepared to break the law and shoot crocodiles that came too close to people, and he had encouraged others in the community to follow his lead. 'If the crocodiles are going to lie on the beach and wait for dogs, or anything, and we see it, we'll shoot it,' he said. Elu said he believed the law that was established to protect crocodiles from extinction was outdated and needed changing to allow culling. 'They can sue us, but it's got to the stage where we think it's the crocodiles or us,' he said.

Over the next several months more dogs disappeared and a 3.5-metre crocodile had made, according to Sergeant Crawford, 'a real nuisance of itself' by following dinghies and lurking near people fishing around the wharf. Shots had been fired at the animal, but it evaded injury or capture.

Three months after Cassey Bond died, a crocodile attacked an officer of the Australian Army's 51st Far North Queensland Regiment during training in the area. The soldier was dragged by the foot to the water's edge at Crystal Creek but managed to escape. Rumours of a crocodile 7.6 metres long persisted in the region, prompting authorities to warn locals and visitors to be wary of camping near waterways.

In September 1995, a large crocodile attacked a nine-year-old girl while she was fishing with her family at Injinoo Point, near the mouth of Cowal Creek, not far from the Jardine River. The girl was about to retrieve a fishing hook she had left on a rock at the water's edge when the crocodile lunged at her with its mouth open. The terrified girl escaped by scrambling backwards as her family rushed to her rescue.

In March 2008, a 3.6-metre crocodile was trapped by wildlife officers in Cowal Creek, just 10 metres from the Injinoo State School fence, where 50 students reguarly congregate to play. Less than three weeks later, a 4.5-metre monster, described by local police as 'lively and aggressive', was captured in the same spot. The 3.6-metre animal was radio tagged and released for scientific purposes, while the larger crocodile was transported to Cairns by barge and sold to a wildlife farm.

The captured crocodile that was believed to have killed Cassey Bond was eventually relocated to a private crocodile breeding farm at Babinda, south of Cairns.

15 GRAHAM FREEMAN: 'I SAW THE TERROR IN HIS EYES'

Almost two years after a five-metre crocodile named Gregory severed and swallowed an attendant's arm at Mick Tabone's Johnstone River Crocodile Farm at Innisfail (see Chapter 17), another handler was attacked in a horrifyingly similar incident, this time with fatal consequences. On Sunday, 27 November 1994, at about 11.15 am, with Tabone absent from the farm, Graham Freeman was mauled to death by a saltwater crocodile after it attacked and dragged him underwater in the fearsome 'death roll'. It was Freeman's 27th birthday. This time the attacker wasn't Gregory, but the next biggest crocodile at the farm, a 4.1-metre animal known as Russell, named after the Russell River where he was captured seven years previously.

Freeman, an experienced handler who had worked with crocodiles in the Northern Territory, was crouching by the side of the pool, answering questions and explaining crocodile behaviour to a group of tourists. When Freeman nudged the animal's head with a rake, a tactic sometimes used to get a crocodile to open its mouth, it struck without warning, grabbing him by the arm and upper body and, in a single movement, twisting him backwards into the water. Freeman had no chance. Tourists screamed as he desperately tried to regain his feet in the last fading seconds of his life.

Shocked into action, Stan Spearman from the nearby town of Tully, his son Michael, 23, and daughter Lynda's partner, Edwin Kirker, 39, rushed through the unlocked gate and frantically tried to save the handler's life. Michael Spearman grabbed a steel fence picket and furiously attacked the crocodile. 'I was hitting hard enough to kill a man but I might as well have been hitting it with a teaspoon,' Spearman told a crowded media conference the day after the attack. Stan Spearman, 61, said the three men tried several times to drag Freeman to safety. 'I had his ankle at one stage and Michael and I were both pulling him towards us, but when the crocodile felt the movement it just started rolling again.'

At the height of the drama, hearing screams, Mick Tabone's wife, Margaret, rushed into the enclosure with a single-barrel shotgun and just one cartridge. Edwin Kirker grabbed the gun and fired at the crocodile, but it had little or no effect. Kirker, an accountant who lived in London with Lynda Spearman, said the couple had only been in the area for two days and were sightseeing with Lynda's family when the tragedy occurred. In a revealing and personal interview one week after Spearman's death, Kirker graphically recounted the events as they unfolded on that fateful day.

> The croc was in the water, but he [Freeman] was crouching down and he couldn't see it. Then it was up and out [of the pool] and it had him. He tried to stand up, but it had him by the left arm, and he slipped. He was barefoot. He tried to pull away. Children were screaming. I dropped my camera and headed for the gate. I grabbed his rake, but he was already in the water. Mick and Stan came in and Mick hit it with a star picket. It rolled two or three times. At first, he was conscious, then it got another grip. He never made a sound. It had him by the head and when he stopped moving, the crocodile stopped, too. I had to load the gun and I got to within two feet of the thing. I shot it in the head, between the eyes, while he was still in its mouth. The croc was still alive.
>
> When the ambulance arrived, I went in again and hooked the rake in the guy's watch to try and pull him out. The crocodile was moving and we had no space behind us. It was lucky we weren't taken, too, but you just don't think, there was no time to think.
>
> He should have had spiked shoes. If he hadn't slipped, he might have got away. We got in there in a couple of seconds, but it had him in the water. He was struggling until it got him by the head.

Lynda Spearman said Graham Freeman was talking directly to her when the crocodile struck.

> He was looking straight at me and I saw the terror in his eyes when the crocodile grabbed him. We're very, very upset about what happened. He was a lovely fellow, kind and interesting. We don't believe the farm should be shut down, but people should be made more aware of the dangers, working with these animals.

When the police arrived, the crocodile was in the pond with Freeman's body partly submerged beside it. Senior Constable Grant Steele said he sent out a call for a high-powered rifle when he realised there was no alternative but to shoot the crocodile.

> The croc was so aggressive we had to take a certain course of action and that was to shoot it. My colleague and I were very concerned and felt frustrated we could not assist the man sooner, but it wasn't to be. I was hoping to Christ I wouldn't miss. It was a pretty hair-raising time.

The first shot appeared to be fatal, but to make certain, three more rounds were fired into the rogue crocodile before Freeman's body was pulled from the pond. Ambulance officers treated four children and several adults who were traumatised by the attack, some of them hysterical and near collapse.

Mick Tabone later described Freeman as a likeable young man who had studied the biology and habits of crocodiles. He had worked at the farm for six months. A post-mortem examination revealed Freeman had died within seconds from severe head and other injuries.

On Thursday, 5 October 1995, Mick and Margaret Tabone faced the Innisfail Magistrates Court charged with breaches of the Queensland Workplace Health and Safety Act. It was alleged the Tabones had failed to meet their obligations of providing a safe workplace, leading to a serious injury causing death. But Margaret Tabone told the court she had specifically warned Freeman not to enter any enclosures while her partner Mick was absent from the farm. In his evidence, Mick Tabone insisted his workplace was safe at that time and he had personally instructed Freeman in crocodile handling for a month before allowing him to conduct tours at the farm. Tabone said he had consistently taught Freeman how to approach crocodiles and warned him against touching them.

Defence counsel John Vandeleur said Margaret Tabone's evidence that she instructed handlers not to enter crocodile pens while her husband was away was uncontested, and that a more experienced handler present at the time would not have saved Freeman's life. Vandeleur told presiding magistrate Clive Williamson that Mick Tabone provided ongoing training and lectures for his staff, especially in handling and safety procedures, and that he kept emergency equipment, including a shotgun, ropes and poles, in a shed adjoining the perimeter fence. Vandeleur told the hushed court nothing could have saved Freeman from almost instantaneous death.

On 31 October, the charges against the Tabones were dismissed by Williamson, who said the prosecution had not proved its case beyond reasonable doubt, and the defendants had taken such measures as were practicable to provide and maintain a safe working environment. He said while safety equipment on the fatal day could have been more accessible, the manner and speed of the attack meant the equipment would not have prevented Freeman's death, and it was not practicable to have armed crocodile handlers close to tourists.

In November 2007, Mick and Margaret Tabone sold their crocodile farm. Mick said he planned to retire, operations to his knee had slowed him down. He said that scars on his body included one on the back of his leg where a crocodile grabbed him in the Johnstone River, and another on his hand left by a farm crocodile after Mick 'accidently hit him on his top jaw as I walked past. They both let me go and I'm left with organic tattoos,' he added.

16 BARRY JEFFERIES: DEATH STRIKES SWIFTLY

It started as a relaxing canoe trip for Townsville couple Barry Jefferies and his wife Glenda as they calmly paddled on the Normanby River in the late afternoon of 16 August 2005. The couple were enjoying the serenity of day's end in the peaceful environment of Lakefield National Park, 150 kilometres north-west of Cooktown. It was a camping and fishing destination they had regularly visited for several years.

In the same national park 10 months beforehand, grandmother Alicia Sorohan created world headlines when she jumped on a crocodile's back to save fellow camper Andrew Kerr from certain death (see Chapter 23). The attack was a reminder that Cape York Peninsula is crocodile territory and extremely dangerous for the unwary.

Jefferies, a 60-year-old railway worker, and his wife were paddling in a scrub-lined section of the river known as

Midway Waterhole, their red plastic canoe in bright contrast to their surroundings in the evening glow of approaching sunset. Hoping for a lucky catch, the couple trailed a baited fishing line behind the vessel. That decision was the most likely single factor that led to Barry Jefferies' tragic death.

At about 5 pm, without warning, a large saltwater crocodile leapt from the water, grabbed Jefferies by the arm, and pulled him out of the canoe. The vessel capsized as he desperately tried to fight off the animal with a paddle, but in seconds he disappeared beneath the water's surface. Jefferies was a big man, fit and strong, but he was no match for the crocodile. The man, nicknamed Harry Butler by his family because of his passion for camping in the wild, was never seen again.

Almost numb with shock, but uninjured, Glenda Jefferies frantically struck out for the bank. With no sign of her husband, she drove 20 minutes to the Lakefield ranger station and raised the alarm. Five park rangers rushed to the spot but, although the canoe was recovered in the darkness, there was no sign of Jefferies' body, or a crocodile.

The next day rangers shot a four-metre crocodile believed to be the killer. It was a known resident of the waterhole, nicknamed Midway by traditional owners of the area. Caretaker of the area, Michael Ross, said the 400-kilogram crocodile had lived in and around the water hole for nearly 30 years and was carefully left alone by locals. 'That old fellow has been there since the early 1970s and it makes me feel a bit sad to see him gone, but he did the wrong thing and had to go. There's crocodiles in all the waterholes, so you can't take risks.'

Ross said he and his family often camped at Midway Waterhole, but were vigilant knowing the crocodile was somewhere nearby. 'He liked his territory and he liked to circle around and let you know it was his territory. If he came too close we would just pack up and leave.'

The search for Jefferies' remains continued. Three days after he disappeared into the waterhole, police and park rangers found his torn shirt and shorts caught in reeds near a large crocodile slide mark on the bank opposite to where the attack took place. One day later, a human thigh bone was found by searchers almost a kilometre north of the attack scene. That bone was all that was recovered from the body of Barry Jefferies. Cape Crocodile had claimed another victim.

In an ironic twist to this human tragedy, Barry and Glenda Jefferies were outspoken opponents of culling crocodiles, believing the animals should be left alone in their natural environment. Following a surge of calls to shoot saltwater crocodiles in the wake of the attack on Andrew Kerr at Bathurst Bay in October 2004, Glenda Jefferies wrote to the *Townsville Bulletin* newspaper condemning the public's reaction. 'An isolated incident in an isolated area of the North has the usual bunch of crocodile experts, ex-shooters and pollies calling for a cull,' she wrote.

> Who would benefit most from the trophy-hunting and culling of crocodiles? A sensible assessment of the situation is more worthy than the sensational outcry that culling would save human lives. Most Australians never venture into these remote areas, and those who do know that preparation needs to be taken. The current call is for a relaxation

of firearm bans in national park areas, and while this has some merit, it is ironic that firearms can take more lives in one year than decades of crocodile attacks.

It was a passionate plea for the continuing protection of one of the world's most dangerous animals. Sadly, just a few months later, one of these animal was to take her husband's life.

PART 3:
GREAT ESCAPES

17 THE TERROR OF EUBENANGEE SWAMP

He was the scourge of a wildlife reserve near Babinda, 60 kilo-metres south of Cairns. He was a five-metre rogue crocodile and he had ruled the coastal waterways of Eubenangee Swamp for years, attacking and killing more than 50 head of cattle and regularly menacing farmers and others who were foolish enough to stray into his kingdom.

In 1989, crocodile farmer Mick Tabone was called in to trap the rampaging animal, known by locals as the 'Terror of Eubenangee Swamp'. It took Tabone and his team six months to finally corner the one-tonne giant in the Alice River, and transport him back to the Johnstone River Crocodile Farm at Innisfail. Named Gregory, after the manager of the property where he was captured, the crocodile became the star attraction at the farm, with Tabone daily sitting on his back, posing for camera-toting tourists.

Then, at 3.20 pm, on Wednesday, 3 February 1993, the unthinkable happened. It was feeding time for Gregory and crocodile handlers, Mark Russell and Darren Cassidy, were inside the enclosure about to perform the feeding ritual in front of half a dozen fascinated tourists watching through the fence. Cassidy was an experienced handler but Russell, 25, originally from Western Australia, had only been employed at the farm for five weeks. While Cassidy tossed a chicken to a crocodile in an adjoining enclosure, Russell walked over to where Gregory was lying in the bottom of his empty concrete pond.

Without warning, the crocodile lunged, grabbing Russell by the left elbow and pulling him down into the pond. As the horrified tourists watched dumbstruck, Gregory went into the notorious crocodile 'death roll'. Russell said later he tried to spread his body out after the first roll, but the animal kept going, twisting his arm off just below the shoulder and swallowing it whole.

Cassidy heard Russell scream and leapt into the pond, striking the crocodile with a rake in an attempt to pull his mate clear. Hearing cries, Tabone rushed to the pen and helped Cassidy get Russell out of the enclosure and into the park's entrance, where they kept the injured man calm until an ambulance arrived. Russell was airlifted to the Cairns Base Hospital where he underwent emergency surgery and was placed in intensive care.

Russell later told reporters he remembered putting his arm out before the attack, but doesn't know why he did that. 'People said I was reaching out to pat him but that wasn't the case. It was a natural reflex, it was self-defence. You see something like that coming at you, then you do it.'

Mick Tabone, however, said it was unlikely the crocodile would have realised he was attacking a human, more likely—because it was feeding time—he had mistaken Russell's extended arm for food.

> It was just one of those unfortunate accidents. Gregory mistook his arm for a piece of meat and it happened. The crocodile doesn't know he's eaten a piece of human—it's not his fault. Gregory was only doing what crocodiles normally do—defend themselves and look for food.

Russell recovered quickly and adopted a philosophical attitude to the horrendous attack that almost took his life, rejecting calls to destroy the crocodile before it harms somebody else. 'It was an accident and killing Gregory wouldn't change anything,' he said. But the nightmare was still in his mind. During the attack he remained conscious and remembered the moment of terror when he stared into Gregory's eyes.

> When he had my arm and pulled me down, my face was just inches from his jaw. Crocodiles have a slit, like cat's eyes, but when he had me the pupils were dilated and looked like human eyes. Then, when he rolled me, his eyes closed. I still get a bit shaky when I talk about it. It was like staring death in the face.

Gregory survived the public backlash against him over the attack, and worldwide media attention ensured he retained top billing over the 900 of his fellow saurians at the farm.

18 'I THOUGHT I WAS A GONER'

Ron Bakx still breaks out into a cold sweat as he recalls the dark night he went for a swim and ended up fighting for his life when a three-metre saltwater crocodile grabbed him by the head and shoulder and tried to death roll him into deeper water. Bakx, 35, survived the sudden attack in waist-deep water by lashing out with his free arm and refusing to panic, even though he was living every north Queenslander's worst nightmare—being eaten alive in the jaws of Australia's most feared animal. The attack happened at 8.30 pm on Friday, 28 November 1997, at Yorkeys Knob, a popular beachside suburb of Cairns. Bakx managed to make it back to the beach, bleeding from deep bite wounds to his head, back and arm, as his friends watched in horror. 'I thought I was a goner because I knew straight away it was a croc and I wouldn't have much of a chance to get away,' he said.

> I'd dived in and was swimming out when it came at me from the side and grabbed me across the shoulder and tried to drag me under in a death roll. Luckily I managed to get a foothold in the sand, so I was able to lash out and somehow break away.
>
> He had me in his mouth for a few seconds, but I didn't feel any pain, just a crushing sensation. I stumbled as I tried to get back to the beach and thought the croc would get me for sure.

Bakx can't remember screaming for help, but his friends say they heard a 'strange roar' before they realised what was happening. 'That sound had to be coming from me,' Bakx said.

The part-time plant operator and his workmates had been enjoying a few Friday afternoon beers at a local pub, later moving the party down to the beach, where they lit a fire and continued their celebrations. Bakx admitted he'd 'had a few' and his decision to go for a swim at night during the crocodile breeding season wasn't a wise one and he should have known better. 'I've lived up here for 10 years and I know the dangers but I still went in the water, and of course that was a stupid thing to do.'

Bakx was extremely lucky. Apart from deep puncture wounds, lacerations, and the biggest scare of his life, he got away with it.

The regional director of the Department of Environment, Lindsay Delzoppo, agreed that Bakx was 'very lucky to be alive' and announced that attempts were being made to trap

Killer crocodile Russell. [ROBERT REID]

Mick Tabone sitting astride Gregory. [ROBERT REID]

Ron Bakx shows the scars on his back from the crocodile attack. [RUSSELL FRANCIS]

'Heroes' Conrad Gilbert (left) and David Short, who saved Elizabeth Pausa's life. [THE CAIRNS POST]

Alicia and Bill Sorohan with grandchildren Kaitlyn and Rhiannan at Cairns Base Hospital. [ALICIA SOROHAN]

GASHED: Two huge toothmarks. Picture: Aaron Curran

RELIEVED: Fishermen Steve Pye (left) and Kel Luscombe examine the croc bite holes in their boat.

Mates tell of lucky escape

EXCLUSIVE

By Simon Cameron

TWO Cairns fishermen yesterday told how they escaped from the jaws of a monster crocodile after it attacked their boat during a fishing trip north of Cooktown last week.

The croc, which they estimated to be at least 5m long, stalked the pair for several minutes before launching a vicious attack which left two gaping holes in the side and bottom of their 4.2m boat.

Kel Luscombe and Stephen Pye, who returned from their trip on Monday, were trolling at the time of the attack, which took place near Frenchman's Reef in the northern part of Princess Charlotte Bay.

But just as quickly as the croc attacked, it disappeared, leaving a stunned pair of fishermen with a boat filling quickly with water and 2km offshore.

Mr Luscombe yesterday described the events leading up to the attack, saying how he tried to steer the boat away from the rogue animal only to have it keep following them.

"He appeared to angle towards us," Mr Luscombe said. "We were doing 8-10 knots and he was keeping up with us easily. He just kept cruising over a bit."

● Continued Page 2

Newspaper article showing close-up of the hull of a boat with two toothmarks and Steve Pye and Kel Luscombe examining the damage. [THE CAIRNS POST]

The crocodile that attacked campers, wounding Alicia Sorohan, and was killed by Jason Sorohan. [THE CAIRNS POST]

Errol Thomas saved his dog JD from a crocodile in a tributary of the Endeavour River, Cooktown. [THE CAIRNS POST]

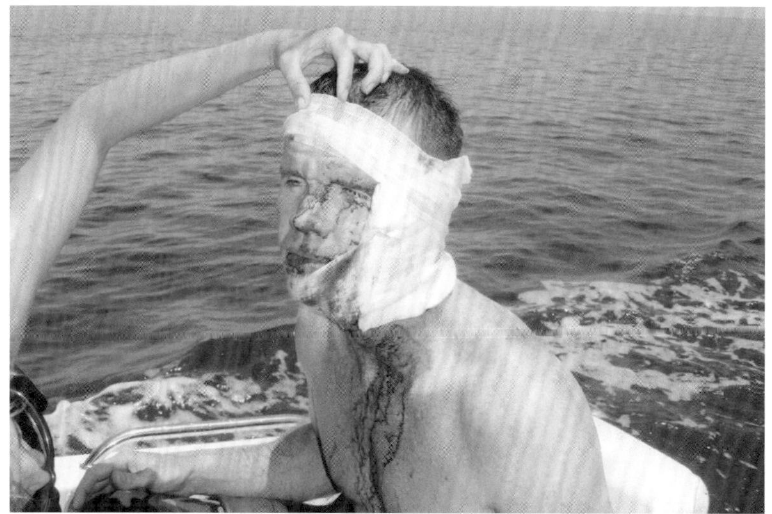

Police Sergeant Jeff Tanswell was attacked by a crocodile in Torres Strait, 8 January 2007. [Jeff Tanswell]

A headless crocodile after being attacked with a chainsaw in 1994. [Dave Donald]

Madeline Tabone with her bridesmaid 'Little Girl'. [ROBERT REID]

Tony Jones, a crocodile handler by day, entertainer by night. [RUSSELL FRANCIS]

David Martin standing on the crocodile believed to be Beryl Wruck's killer. Richard Ralph (behind Martin) does not agree. [Richard Ralph]

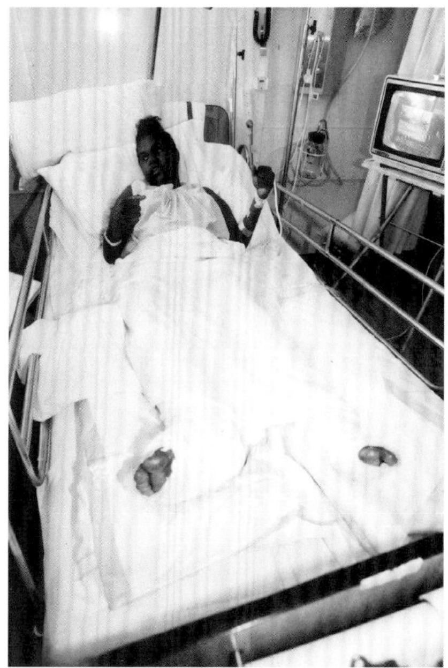

Elizabeth Pausha in hospital after the attack on her at Chinaman Creek. [The Cairns Post]

Oscar and his handler George Craig in 1986. [Robert Reid]

the animal and either relocate it or destroy it. 'Crocodile attacks on beaches are totally unacceptable and if necessary we'd shoot the animal,' he said.

Hartley's Creek Crocodile Farm manager, Geoff McClure, said Bakx had been dicing with death by going in the water at night. 'This bloke did everything wrong by swimming in a croc habitat, at night, and during the mating season,' he said. 'He was also outside the protected stinger net enclosure. Had it been a larger croc, he'd have been gone for sure.'

But Bakx was philosophical about his brush with death, refusing to blame the crocodile for his near demise. 'I was in the croc's territory, so I was fair game and it's only luck that I'm standing here today,' he said.

Twelve days after the attack, a three-metre crocodile believed to be the culprit was harpooned by rangers at nearby Thomatis Creek and relocated to the Cairns Crocodile Farm, south of the city. He was promptly named Baxter, in honour of his intended victim, and released into his new environment. Ron Bakx agreed to media requests for a second encounter with the crocodile, but this time from a safe distance, and only if he could take along a beer to calm his nerves.

He said while the highly publicised incident had kept him busy with interviews from all over the world, he still had quiet moments when he reflected on just how close he was to death. 'I got a fright after a bad dream the other night, which made me realise how serious it all was. It was a close call and a clear warning to others not to swim at night in the ocean, especially at this time of the year.'

Farm manager Andrew Young said Baxter would enjoy celebrity status in his own pool with a plaque explaining the circumstances of the attack and his subsequent capture.

Bakx's friends said they intended to celebrate their mate's lucky escape by holding a 'croc party' each month at the same spot where he almost met his death. 'But I won't be going swimming,' Bakx said.

19 ESCAPE AT CHINAMAN CREEK

Friday, 6 February 1998, was a typical summer's day in tropical Cairns, and by nightfall the hot and steamy conditions had barely abated. It was the middle of the wet season and locals were used to the oppressive heat at this time of the year. They put up with it and cooled off the best way they could.

At Chinaman Creek, just four kilometres from the heart of the tourist city, 18-year-old Elizabeth Pausa was partying with a group of relatives and friends at a permanent squatter's camp on the banks of the tidal creek. All-night drinking sessions were common at the campsite, a popular meeting place for indigenous people from communities all over Cape York. Swimming in the creek, night and day, was a normal activity and nobody gave it a second thought.

At about 7.40 pm, Pausa moved from a concrete block, where she had been sitting, into the shallows of the creek to splash her face with water. In an instant, a saltwater crocodile had her by the legs and was dragging her into deeper water. The young woman screamed for help before being pulled off her feet and underwater. Miraculously, she managed to break the surface with her upper body and grab an overhanging branch of a mangrove tree. But the branch snapped under her weight, with the crocodile still clinging to her leg. 'I thought he was going to take me away to where he lived, and I had to stop him taking me there,' she later said from hospital. With strength born of desperation, Pausa managed to lunge for a thicker branch, which held firm as she struggled to break the crocodile's hold.

Alerted by her screams, 14-year-old Conrad Giblet and David Short, 25, rushed to her aid. Giblet quickly climbed out on a tree trunk over the creek and grabbed the woman's hair, while at the same time beating at the crocodile's head with a stick. Short, meantime, had rushed into the water up to his chest and urged Pausa to wrap her arms around him and hang on tight. The heavily built man, known among his friends as 'the big fella', then determinedly started to back out of the creek, with the terrified girl clinging to his body.

Short yelled to Giblet to splash the water with the stick to divert the crocodile's attention. It worked and the crocodile opened its jaws. Short dragged Pausa to safety, where she fainted from shock and loss of blood. Both her legs and one foot were badly mauled and her tracksuit pants had been ripped from her body. It was an act of instinctive bravery by Giblet and Short, and the pair's combined action almost certainly saved Elizabeth Pausa from death.

The day after the attack, Department of Environment rangers trapped a 3.2-metre crocodile in the same area, declaring it publicly to be the crocodile reponsible for the attack. But Giblet, Short and other campers believed the animal was the wrong one, that the real culprit was smaller, around two metres in length.

Speaking from Cairns Base Hospital three days after surgery on both legs and her foot, Pausa said the ordeal had left her with recurring nightmares and chilling visions of the attack. 'It scares me to think about it, but I just can't stop,' she said. 'Whenever I close my eyes I get a fright.' Pausa said she too believed the crocodile was smaller than the 3.2-metre animal caught by rangers. 'If it had been that big I couldn't have got away, I'd have been eaten.'

But the Department of Environment's Lindsay Delzoppo didn't agree his rangers had captured the wrong crocodile, stating it was unlikely a two-metre animal would attack a human with such ferocity. 'I'm not dismissing the claims, and I'm not saying it couldn't happen, but we believe a smaller crocodile would have been too scared to attack like that.'

Cairns Mayor Tom Pyne said although he was grateful the young woman had survived the attack and would fully recover, she should take responsibility for her decision to enter the water. 'She was doing everything wrong by dangling her feet in the water where there were food scraps in the creek from people washing cooking utensils,' he said.

'For years we have been warning people not to clean fish on boat ramps, not to toss food scraps in the water, not to wade in tidal streams and certainly not to swim, or even paddle, in known crocodile habitats.'

Pausa defended her actions, saying people regularly swam in the creek, and she had not thought it was dangerous, but she would never go in the water again at night. 'That would be too scary,' she said.

Incredibly, the day after the attack that almost took Pausa's life, a group of adults and children—including Conrad Giblet—were back swimming and diving for mussels in Chinaman Creek. Lindsay Delzoppo called on people at the campsite to stay out of the water as reports of other big crocodiles in the creek, a tributary of the open waters of Trinity Inlet, were being treated seriously, and rangers were patrolling the waterways. 'It is borderline insanity to swim there. Please don't do it,' he said.

Two weeks after the attack, Elizabeth Pausa was transferred from Cairns Base Hospital to Brisbane Royal Hospital where she endured a series of painful skin grafts on the deep teeth marks in her foot and ankle. It took another five weeks of rehabilitation before she fully recovered from her ordeal.

On 23 March, a three-metre crocodile was trapped in a baited cage in Chinaman Creek, one of more than 50 mature crocodiles estimated to inhabit the waterways of Trinity Inlet.

In September, Conrad Giblet and David Short received national bravery awards from the Queensland Governor at a ceremony in Cairns for their heroic rescue of the young woman.

The crocodile believed to be responsible for the attack was transported to George Craig's Marineland Melanesia wildlife park on Green Island. Craig said the crocodile was appropriately named Trinity and was a popular tourist attraction, but it was a dangerous animal that needed to be watched carefully. 'He's a feisty animal and not to be trusted,' Craig said.

20 A FRIGHT FOR TALEESHA

It may well have been only a small specimen, but the crocodile that attacked eight-year-old Taleesha Fegatilli on north Queensland's Four Mile Beach left her with a big fright and serious puncture wounds to her body after an innocent swim with her siblings turned into a nightmare. The Atherton schoolgirl was frolicking in shallow water with her twin brother Jordain and older sister Karina, 11, at the southern end of the world-famous beach when the attack occurred. It was around 10.15 am on Sunday, 30 September 2001, and the Fegatilli family, along with hundreds of other locals and tourists, was enjoying the day on the broad, sweeping beach that is the main drawcard for the waterfront town of Port Douglas, an hour's drive north of Cairns.

Bruno Fegatilli said they had only been on the beach for a few minutes. The attack on his daughter happened so quickly he didn't see the crocodile, but when he heard her screams he rushed into the water to rescue her. 'I was only a few metres away and I could see she was cut badly,' he later said. 'I thought I had lost her at one stage when I had her in my arms and she was bleeding all over me.' The girl had a deep gash on her right arm and wounds to her leg, abdomen and shoulder.

Mariel Visee, a tourist from Rotterdam, was sunbaking when she heard the commotion. 'I heard screaming from the water and looked up as the father rushed out carrying the little girl,' she said. 'I didn't see the crocodile, but after all that I wasn't going in for a swim.'

Queensland Parks and Wildlife Service manager, Dr Mark Read, said Taleesha confirmed she had seen a 'shadow' in the water that was most definitely a crocodile, which he estimated was between 1.5 metres and 2.5 metres in length. 'She was paddling on a boogie board and it's likely the crocodile accidentally brushed her and lashed out with either a single bite or a couple of quick bites as a natural reaction,' he said. 'It was probably a case of misadventure—the crocodile was startled and had no malicious intent.' Perhaps not, but Taleesha was fortunate she was in shallow water and the crocodile wasn't the same one that had made Four Mile Beach its home for several years.

In November 1996, a three-metre crocodile entertained tourists as it 'surfed' the waves in the same area that Taleesha suffered her frightening attack. The crocodile in 1996 drew a large crowd of beachgoers who photographed the animal just metres offshore for three hours before it swam away in the direction of nearby Mowbray River. The crocodile was sighted many times over the next five years, including several times in the months leading up to the attack on Taleesha. Despite efforts by wildlife rangers to trap the animal, it eluded capture.

Douglas Shire Mayor Mike Berwick said he was concerned that crocodiles living in close proximity to humans represented a tragedy waiting to happen. 'I don't want to scare people needlessly—and I might add you're more likely to get mugged on the streets of Cairns than attacked by a crocodile—but what if a child is killed on Four Mile Beach and we hadn't taken enough measures to prevent it?'

Berwick said if all other efforts to keep crocodiles away from human habitation failed, then they should be shot on sight. 'They have to be kept away from boat ramps and beaches and if they come back they get the bullet. You can't muck around, they're not welcome near people.'

21 'HE WAS BIGGER THAN THE BOAT'

Kel Luscombe and Steve 'Chilli' Pye escaped with their lives, and they have a photograph to prove it, after a huge crocodile attacked their boat while cruising two kilometres offshore in Princess Charlotte Bay. The two Cairns mates were on a 10-day fishing trip in the northern part of the bay, well known as a crocodile hotspot and the scene of several attacks in recent years.

It was a calm October day in 2002 and the men were trolling along a sand cay near Frenchman Reef in their 4.2-metre aluminium dory. The water was crystal-clear and nothing seemed amiss. They were experienced fishermen and knew the area well. It was getting on in the day and they were looking forward to heading back to shore to cook up a fresh fish dinner and have a few beers around the campfire. At about 2 pm they noticed a shape in the water about

40 metres away. 'We didn't know what it was at first,' Luscombe said. 'But then it kept pace with us and we saw it was a crocodile. He swam parallel with us for a few minutes and then moved closer and closer until suddenly it reared out of the water and went for us.'

Without thinking, Steve Pye grabbed a disposable camera and managed to take a blurred photo of the croc's massive head—seconds before it hit the boat and sunk its teeth into the hull with a force that knocked the boat several metres sideways. 'I got him just before he struck, it was a split-second, one-in-a-million shot,' Pye said. 'I can still see his glistening head and huge jaws. I can particularly remember the big eyes. He was bigger than the boat, so he was over five metres long.'

Luscombe said the shock of the impact almost threw him into the water. 'The noise was horrific when he hit, like a car crash, and I had to hang on. Water started gushing in through the croc's tooth holes. I yelled out, "We're taking water Chilli", and gunned the motor fast.' Pye frantically cut up a potato sack and stuffed pieces in the holes as Luscombe headed the boat 'flat chat' back towards the beach. 'We had a powerful 40hp engine and the speed kept us high in the water as Chilli bailed as fast as he could. We had a bit of luck on our side to make it back in one piece.'

Luscombe said the size of the dory probably saved their lives. 'He would have tipped a 12-footer over, I'm pretty sure of that. I've been fishing up there for 30 years and I've seen a lot of big crocs in that time, but by the size of this bloke's head, he was the biggest.'

Luscombe said it was most likely they had intruded into the crocodile's area and it had reacted instinctively to a perceived threat. 'The sand cay was probably part of his territory and he decided to get rid of us. Well, he did, that's for sure.'

Safe on the beach, but still about 30 kilometres from their camp, the two mates considered their next move. It was simple. 'We cracked open the two cans of beer we had left and just looked at each other in amazement,' Pye said.

An inspection of the dory showed two gaping holes underneath the aluminium hull—the thickest and strongest part of the boat—and a smaller puncture on the side. The two men found teeth fragments embedded in the hull and 'sticky' blood around the holes. They used the empty beer cans to patch the holes in their boat, before cautiously limping back to their campsite. The almost-new boat was later found to be too damaged to be restored to its original safety standards.

Luscombe was asked what crocodile hunter Steve Irwin would have done in a similar situation. 'He would have shit himself the same as we did,' he said.

22 DARING LEAP SAVED SCHOOLGIRL

Schoolgirl Hannah Thompson owes her life to an island resort owner who snatched her from the jaws of a 3.5-metre crocodile in a daring rescue off the east coast of Cape York Peninsula. In April 2004, Hannah, 11, was swimming with friends on a fishing trip at Margaret Bay, 600 kilometres north of Cairns, when a cruising crocodile grabbed her arm and started to pull her under.

Owner and operator of nearby Haggerstone Island Guest House, Roy Turner, leapt from a boat onto the crocodile's back and jammed his finger into the animal's eye, forcing it to open its mouth and free the girl. Turner, a former crocodile hunter, instinctively went into action mode when somebody on the boat yelled 'crocodile!' That was enough for Turner. In a Crocodile Dundee–type feat, he scrambled over two passengers to get to the side of the boat and jumped overboard.

'I saw the shadow of the croc in the water and I immediately thought of Hannah,' Turner later told reporters. He said the crocodile raised its head as he landed on its back. 'I landed exactly where I wanted to land, behind his head. I got a finger in his left eye and straight away he dropped her.'

It was a fishing trip that would certainly have ended in tragedy if not for Turner's quick thinking. The fishing party of three adults and eight children was in shallow, crystal-clear water over a white sandy bottom when the crocodile struck.

Turner played down his role in the drama, insisting his heroic act just happened instinctively, but his experience with crocodiles was an obvious factor that helped save the girl.

> It all happened in a matter of seconds. I was actually stirring a pot on the stove when I heard the screams. I was able to jump right on top of the crocodile and I think that stunned him. Not many people know to go for their eyes, but that is what you have to do—that's the only thing you can do.

Hannah escaped with several puncture wounds to her left arm and lost her watch in the attack. She was flown by helicopter to Thursday Island Hospital to receive treatment. A nine-year-old boy, who was also in the water, was scratched across the back as the crocodile brushed past him. He was quickly pulled to safety by a passenger on the boat as Turner wrestled the crocodile.

The next day a crocodile, believed to have been the attacker, was shot by wildlife rangers within 200 metres of the incident. Its stomach contents were examined, but in a wry twist to the story, Hannah's watch was not found.

23 CROCODILE 'GRANNY' DUNDEE

It was just one more fishing trip to Cape York the group of three families had enjoyed for six consecutive years, trekking north in their convoy of four-wheel-drive vehicles from their homes in Brisbane. This was the annual holiday they all looked forward to, a three-week safari to their favourite camping spot at remote Bathurst Bay, more than 2200 kilometres away from the hustle and bustle of Queensland's capital city.

Alicia Sorohan, 60, and her husband Bill, also 60, were old hands at camping and had been visiting Bathurst Bay with their family on a regular basis for 20 years. On this trip were their adult son Jason and daughter Melinda Clancy, and Melinda's husband Wayne and their daughters Kaitlyn, seven, and four-year-old Rhiannan. Among others on the journey were Jason's workmate, Andrew Kerr, his wife Diane and their three-month-old son Kelly.

The campers set out in late September 2004, fully equipped with food supplies, extra fuel, fishing gear, trail bikes and dinghies. They were experienced in the bush and well prepared for the journey, leaving nothing to chance.

The group set up their campsite of five tents and a separate gazebo and were comfortably settled in at Bathurst Bay by early October. They had timed their trip to avoid the summer monsoon season, locally known as the wet, usually occurring between December and March. The nights were pleasant and the days, although hot, were dry and bearable. The city was forgotten in the serenity of Cape York.

Bathurst Bay faces the Coral Sea, on the outer edge of Princess Charlotte Bay—the mouth-shaped indentation that looks as if it has been bitten out of the Cape's eastern coastline. Bathurst Bay is 300 kilometres north-west of Cairns, and is hemmed in between Cape Melville National Park and Lakefield National Park. It is an idyllic place, far from cities and towns, and revered by nature enthusiasts as an unspoiled location of beauty and tranquillity. It is also a place of great danger, where death lurks in the waterways.

Shortly before dawn on Monday, 11 October, Alicia Sorohan awoke to frantic screams coming from somewhere in the camp. Rushing from her tent she was horrified to see, in the dim light, a huge saltwater crocodile dragging Andrew Kerr by the leg from his tent. Without a thought for her own safety, the slightly built grandmother leapt onto the head of the 300-kilogram animal and hung on grimly while it attempted to drag Kerr to the water's edge, about 50 metres away. It was an instinctive but amazingly heroic action that logic would indicate could only end in tragedy. But luck and quick thinking by her son, Jason, saved both her and Kerr from certain death.

The crocodile—later measured at 4.2 metres—released Kerr, shook its head, and flung Alicia to one side like a rag doll. In the same motion it turned quickly, smashing her face with its head, before grabbing her right arm above the elbow. Jason, who was only seconds behind his mother, immediately jumped on the animal and, in a kneeling position, shot it several times in the back of the head with a handgun. It was good shooting. The crocodile died instantly. Had Jason missed the vital 'kill shot' to the brain, the enraged beast would certainly, at the very least, have ripped his mother's arm off, before continuing its rampage. It was also lucky he had a large-calibre pistol.

Bill Sorohan was next on the frontline, armed with an axe. He had heard someone shouting that a dingo was in the camp and his first thought was for Andrew's infant son, Kelly. Dingoes had been seen in the area when the campers first arrived and they were foremost in Bill's mind. 'It all happened so fast,' he later recounted. 'We heard the screaming and at first we thought it was a dingo. We grabbed a torch and dived out of the tent. My wife thought the croc had the baby and jumped on it.'

Diane Kerr woke to her husband screaming, 'Grab the baby!' as he was dragged out of the tent. She grabbed the bassinette in one arm and held onto Andrew with her other hand, as she 'just screamed and screamed'.

Kelly could have been the crocodile's main target. It had made straight for the Kerr family's tent, ignoring the gazebo stocked with food supplies nearest the water. The huge beast could have heard the baby's cries during the night or merely sensed his presence. It's well known that crocodiles prefer small, vulnerable targets. Fortunately for the child, his father was nearest the tent's entrance and became, instead, the animal's intended victim.

Not far away, Canberra Raiders rugby league player Ben Jones was preparing for a day's fishing with his father and a friend when they were startled by spotlights and loud noises coming through the bush. 'It was our first time up there but I knew something was up and we got over there as quickly as we could. We were the first on the scene and helped out with a bit of first aid.' Jones said the crocodile 'was the biggest thing I had seen in my life. When we got there the croc had been shot dead on the ground and the injured bloke was only two metres from him.' The star second-rower became the subject of wild rumours that it was he who had jumped on the crocodile's back and saved the campers. Consequently, he was dubbed 'Croc' Jones by his teammates, much to his embarrassment. 'Alicia was the one who jumped on the crocodile's head. She is the real hero.'

The crocodile—the size of a standard family vehicle—lay dead in the sand. Alicia Sorohan and Andrew Kerr lay nearby, both seriously injured. The campers were in shock. Their holiday now seemed straight out of a horror movie.

Alicia's arm was almost severed and her facial injuries included severe lacerations and a broken nose. Andrew's mauled leg was badly broken and he had injuries to his arms and upper body.

Bill Sorohan quickly decided to drive his wife overland to the Lakefield National Park ranger station for help—a gruelling five-hour, 125-kilometre journey through some of Australia's roughest terrain. To make matters worse, a bushfire had swept through the area and in places trees had fallen across the bush track. Bill said there were no drugs available to help ease Alicia's pain during the bumpy ordeal. 'We didn't have anything to help her, not even an aspirin,' he said. Bill revealed Alicia's arm was so badly mauled 'you could put your fist in the hole. But she didn't lose consciousness and was talking the whole time, asking about Andrew and the baby, and the other children. She was concerned about everyone except herself, and didn't complain once.'

Andrew Kerr was considered too seriously injured to make the trip and was kept at the camp. An emergency beacon was activated, radio calls were sent out for assistance, and a giant 'SOS' marked out in the sand. A helicopter engaged by the Queensland Parks and Wildlife Service on a feral pig control shooting expedition in the area soon responded and the injured man was also taken to the Lakefield station. The pair was then flown by the Royal Flying Doctor Service to the Cairns Base Hospital for emergency surgery.

Alicia spent 10 days in hospital before being released. Doctors attached two metal plates to her arm bones, using 12 screws to hold it all together.

It was a remarkable act of bravery by Alicia, and a remarkable escape from death for both her and Andrew Kerr. It was unusual behaviour for a crocodile to attack a camp away from the water's edge, but it seems likely that previous visitors to the site had cleaned fish and left remains behind, encouraging the animal to forage for food further up the bank than it normally would. Or it could have been an opportunistic attack, the crocodile deciding instinctively that the smell of food was worth the risk of possible danger.

Dr Mark Read, Queensland Parks and Wildlife Service senior conservation officer, said he suspected previously discarded fish scraps had been the reason for the bold attack. That particular area, however, was not considered dangerous crocodile country because there were no mangroves and it was not near an estuary. 'Crocodiles often travel from one watercourse to the next and use the ocean simply as a crocodile highway, so it's not unusual for them to be swimming along beaches,' he said. 'But I'm certainly wondering why this particular crocodile stopped and made a very conscious decision to head up the beach.'

From her hospital bed, Alicia told reporters jumping on the crocodile was a natural reaction, because she was the first person out of the tent, and she 'would have done the same for anyone'. 'It felt like hitting a brick wall,' she said. 'The crocodile was huge . . . just horrible.'

Alicia was an instant celebrity, but denied she was a hero as depicted by headlines across Australia and media reports around the world. 'I did what I had to do. He was there, he needed help, and I was the first one there,' she modestly explained on a television current affairs program.

In July 2006, Alicia received the Star of Courage in the

annual Australian Bravery Awards. The awards are given 'in recognition of acts of the most conspicuous courage in circumstances of great peril'.

Alicia, still unable to fully use her injured arm, felt honoured by the award but was philosophical about the actions that made her world-famous as 'the crocodile-wrestling granny' from Australia. 'It's just something you do,' she said.

24 'DON'T LET HIM EAT ME!'

It was a case of the violent attacker who got away, but policeman Jeff Tanswell was more than happy to let this offender escape the long arm of the law. The escapee was a saltwater crocodile that grabbed Tanswell by the head as he snorkelled in the tropical waters of Torres Strait. As the crocodile dragged him under, Sergeant Tanswell, in a terrifying moment of chilling clarity, thought he was a dead man. With his consciousness resigned to the fact that his life was over, he knew he had just seconds left.

Then, as he struggled, the crocodile suddenly let him go, and he surfaced. Against all the odds, against all accepted knowledge of crocodile behaviour, the predator had not held him underwater until he drowned, had not then dismembered his body or dragged him off to some distant lair, but had released the hold on his victim and swam off. Jeff Tanswell had somehow escaped with his life.

On Monday, 8 January 2007, Tanswell, 37, his wife Jane, also a police officer, and colleagues Senior Constable David McCarthy and Constable Amanda Jeppesen had a day off from duties at their Thursday Island headquarters. It was a perfect day in paradise and the blue waters of the Strait looked ideal for a fishing and swimming cruise, something the friends had enjoyed many times before.

The party motored in two boats to Little Adolphus Island, one of a group of islands just 15 kilometres directly north of the tip of Cape York Peninsula and about 40 kilometres east of Thursday Island. It was an idyllic place to visit, and the rigours of police work were far from the minds of the relaxed officers.

Tanswell and McCarthy steered their boats around the island 'to see what might be hanging around'. Although the water was flat, calm and crystal-clear, they wanted to make certain no sharks were in the area. Satisfied, McCarthy anchored his boat and he and Jeppesen transferred to Tanswell's craft.

Leaving Jane in charge of the boat, Tanswell donned his wetsuit and snorkelling gear, and entered the water with his two friends. 'Dave and Amanda swam out to the coral edge, about 20 metres away, but I decided to go in closer to the island's bank,' Tanswell said. 'I wasn't keen on the deep water, because I had sharks in the back of my mind.' Sharks, yes, but crocodiles were the last thing on the policeman's mind.

> I was swimming underwater over a sandy patch about five or six metres from the rocky point of the island when whack! I was hit so hard from behind my whole body immediately shut down. The hit was cold, hard and heavy and I lost everything. I had no sensory feedback from my body at all, but my mind was still ticking over. I was like a rag doll, like I was dangling on a string, completely helpless.

In those first, frantic, horrifying two or three seconds, Tanswell's head was in the vice-like grip of a crocodile's jaws and he was being dragged towards the bottom.

> There was this massive pressure and I felt my skull was being crushed. At first I thought something inanimate, like a lump of coral or a log had hit me, but then the crushing pain came in and I knew some kind of animal had me. I started kicking and shoving, fighting for my life. I lashed out with a small spear-gun I was holding tightly in my right hand.

Panic and fear flooded Tanswell's mind as he realised death was merely seconds away. But suddenly, inexplicably, the pressure was off and his head released.

He shot to the surface, gasping for air. He looked around, straight into the eyes of the crocodile. Wildly, he thrashed the spear-gun in the water.

> I remember yelling to Jane, 'Get here now! Get here now!' and screaming out to the others, 'Croc in the water! Croc in the water!' My mind was saying 'calm down, calm down, keep it together, don't let him eat me.' I felt completely helpless, entirely at the mercy of this animal.

Then the crocodile, estimated to be about 2.5 metres long, was gone and Tanswell was alive, joining the select list of attack victims who lived to tell their tale.

On the boat, Jane Tanswell saw what looked like 'a croc's head on a stick' poking out of the water. Thinking 'that can't be a crocodile', she instinctively started the motor, just as her husband's head broke the surface. Fighting to stay calm she headed for him and hauled him on board by his wetsuit, followed quickly by McCarthy and Jeppesen, who had both heard their friend scream but didn't realise he'd been attacked. Just in case, McCarthy had loaded his heavy-duty spear-gun while in the water, and saw the crocodile swimming towards him before veering sharply away.

Tanswell had a deep tooth puncture in his left cheek, part of his ear torn off, and lacerations to his head and neck. He later had 17 stitches in his wounds and micro-surgery to repair his ear. 'Jane was shaking so much, she couldn't bandage me up from the first-aid kit, so Amanda did the job until we got to hospital.'

As Tanswell said, he 'got off lightly', possibly due to the fact the crocodile acted in defence of its territory, and not out of hunger.

> I'm 186 centimetres tall, and in the wetsuit and fins I'd look much bigger, probably like a crocodile in his territory, so he's had a go at me. He could have snapped my neck or crushed my head, so it wasn't a hunger motivated attack, that's for sure, or he would have had me.

The police officer's story attracted international media attention, and the Queensland Police Union jumped in to help Tanswell negotiate a cheque-book deal. The Nine Network secured a television and magazine exclusive for an undisclosed sum, believed to be in the 'tens of thousands' of dollars.

But not everybody was happy the group had been visiting Adolphus Island in the first place. Traditional owners of the Adolphus group of islands said the crocodile was part of the spirit of the area and it was disrespectful for anyone to intrude, except for Aboriginal custodians.

Isaac Savage, secretary of the Muri Land Trust, said it was 'suicide' to visit the islands without permission from the owners because it was a sacred site and 'terrible things always happen' if that respect is violated. He said Jeff Tanswell was lucky to escape with his life. 'It was not a smart move on his part. Everybody in the Torres Strait knows that's a no-go zone.' Savage said indigenous people lived in the area without fear of crocodiles.

> My son swims all day until 11 o'clock at night and that croc could be floating 60 or 80 metres away. There's crocodiles all over that place and they don't worry us. That crocodile lives 100 metres away from where we camp. He has always been there ever since I was a kid. To us he is like a countryman.

But Jeff Tanswell said it had been an innocent trip and he didn't feel he had been breaking any traditional law by visiting the island. 'It's ironic, but indigenous locals that very morning told us to go out there because we'd get a good crayfish for dinner,' he said.

Tanswell said it took six months before he was confident enough to get back in the water.

> Jane is completely off the idea of water now, but although I'm back diving, it's different, that beauty and magic of being underwater has gone for me. It feels like lost innocence in a way. I'm now in a constant primal state of fear, thinking something out there will get me, that any minute now I could be next in the food chain.

25 MORE GREAT ESCAPES

Stories of crocodile escapes abound in the folklore of Cape York Peninsula. Some are true, some are not, and sometimes fact and fantasy blend into adventure yarns that cannot be verified one way or another. Just as it is impossible to know how many humans have died from crocodile attacks since the early days of white settlement, so too is it impossible to know the number of genuine escapes. In the 19th century and the first half of the 20th century, many disappearances and deaths were not reported to authorities due to the extreme isolation of the early settlers. Communication was difficult, slow, and often not worth the effort. The hardy breed of pioneers of those days buried their dead, mourned those who disappeared, and tended to their wounds the best they could. Sometimes, word filtered out of the bush that someone had been taken by a crocodile, or had miraculously escaped, but more often than not the outside world didn't hear of such incidents.

Aboriginal people, as skilled as they were in bushcraft, also fell victim to sudden death from crocodiles as they hunted and gathered in their ancient homeland. Most went unreported. If they were severely wounded, they died. That was the way it was.

But in recent years, many authentic cases of humans escaping from the fearsome predators in north Queensland have been documented. Previous chapters told some of those remarkable stories. Here are a few more of them.

In March 1993, Silver Plains cattle station hand Michael Taylor, 24, and his workmate Peter van Stratten were attempting to float a four-wheel-drive motorbike across a freshwater creek when Taylor felt a 'bit of a whack' on his foot. He didn't feel any pain and thought his foot was caught in debris at the bottom of the murky waterway. 'But then my foot started going backwards and I knew what it was,' he said later. 'The croc had my leg in its mouth up to my knee.'

In waist-deep water, Taylor managed to grab the animal's jaw and tried to force its mouth open, cutting his fingers in the process. Fortunately for Taylor, this was one of those times when a crocodile suddenly decides to let its victim go, and released his leg. Van Stratten helped his mate to the bank and then ran five kilometres to the station homestead, jumped in a vehicle and sped back along the track, where he met Taylor gamely limping home.

The two men had been repairing fences damaged by recent floodwaters when they entered the creek. Van Stratten had crossed safely and returned to help take the bike across. He was pulling from the front, with Taylor pushing from behind when the crocodile struck. Taylor received 20 teeth puncture marks in his leg and calf, and deep scratches to his ankle.

Silver Plains station is situated 40 kilometres from Coen and close to the coast of Princess Charlotte Bay, the location of many crocodile attacks.

In the first week of January 1996, Jeff Callander got an unwelcomed New Year's present when a two-metre freshwater crocodile—a species not known for attacking humans—took a liking to his arm during a camping trip near Georgetown, 400 kilometres south-west of Cairns. Callander, 35, a well-known Cairns Australian Rules football player, was attacked while swimming across the Einasleigh River, about 40 kilometres from Georgetown. 'I decided to swim back to where our vehicles were after walking along the river in search of a better camping spot,' he said. During the swim, in the middle of a deep pool, he felt something—which he thought was a big fish—'chomp' his hand. 'But when it really clamped down hard I naturally reefed my hand out of the water and found myself staring eye to eye with a big freshie,' he said.

Callander had a flash of memory from his days playing football in the Northern Territory, when locals had advised him to always poke an attacking crocodile in the eyes. Good advice, if you can get away with it. But Callander decided to go one step further. 'I clenched a fist and gave it a clout between the eyes,' he said.

The crocodile let go and Callander quickly grabbed his dog, which had been swimming behind him, and threw it on the bank, before 'kicking and splashing' his way out of the water, where he bound his arm with his T-shirt and walked back to camp. His wife, a nurse, treated his wounds, which included deep lacerations to one finger and an almost-severed tendon in another. He later required surgery in Cairns to repair the wounds.

Callander said his friends saw the funny side of the attack and gave him no sympathy. 'When I came out of the operation there was a huge picture of a crocodile on my bed, and people have been sending me crocodile warning signs!'

Just nine weeks later, a marine biologist also used the 'bash a croc' technique to escape from a four-metre saltwater crocodile while scuba diving off Cape York Peninsula's east coast. The giant crocodile attacked Dr Tony Ayling while he was on a scientific dive at Cape Flattery, about 140 kilometres north of Cooktown.

The Daintree-based biologist was underwater measuring coral growths with another diver at 10 am when the crocodile lunged at him from behind, grabbing his foot firmly in its jaws. It was 23 February 1996, the scientist's 49th birthday, but the force of the bite made him think it was to be his last and he would be dead in seconds. 'It was incredible—it felt like my foot was jammed in a vice. For a few seconds I thought, "This is it. I'm done for."'

Ayling said he 'bashed' the crocodile's eyes with a surveying stick and—incredibly—managed to grab the animal's front legs and wrap them up and around his back in a manoeuvre that had many experienced crocodile handlers later shaking their heads in amazement. 'His front legs were quite weak, surprisingly,' Ayling said, 'and I don't think he liked the exertion of the struggle, because after several minutes he just took off really fast.'

Realising he was free, Ayling swam 'flat out' to his boat, about 20 metres away, and banged on its side to warn the other diver, who was unaware of the attack due to the murky water. But on board the boat, Ayling's wife, Avril, had watched the drama unfold with a sense of impending doom. 'He was propelled out of the water up to his rib cage. He yelled at me to start the motor and then he disappeared under the water again,' she said later, describing the attack. 'It was just horrific. I thought that would be the last time I would see him. Not many people survive crocodile attacks. It seemed like a million years, like it was happening in slow motion.'

Ayling spent a week in Cairns Base Hospital recovering from three bite wounds to his foot that required 26 stitches. The biologist said he had been diving for 34 years and this was the first time he'd had a 'close encounter' with a crocodile and would be more selective in his future choices of dive sites.

* * *

Crocodiles like dogs, and attacks on dogs are common throughout north Queensland. Most canines smell danger and stay well clear of a waterway when there's a crocodile nearby, but some ignore their natural instinct and venture too close for comfort. Some escape from their lapse of judgement, but most don't, and end up providing the saurians with a tasty meal that's just the right size and poses no threat to their own safety. Occasionally a dog survives because a human intervenes, risking his or her own life to save man's best friend.

In March 1999, Cooktown man Errol Thomas created international news when he wrestled a crocodile barehanded to save his dog in a tributary of the Endeavour River. Thomas, 43, and a friend were about to go for a swim about 2 pm when the two-metre saltwater crocodile grabbed the dog, a Brazilian bull mastiff female named JD, and dragged it underwater.

Even though the Endeavour River region is well known for its large crocodile population, the water was running fast on that day and Thomas 'thought we'd be right'. They weren't, but fortunately for them JD went in for a dip first. 'I saw JD's head disappear under the water and he [Thomas's friend] yelled out that a croc had my dog,' Thomas said. Thomas leapt into the waist-deep water and clutched at the crocodile, which had the struggling dog firmly in its mouth as it headed for a deeper part of the river. Thomas then had a desperate running battle with the crocodile over 50 metres as it tried to escape with its prey.

> I was in hot pursuit and the only thing I could think of to stop the croc was to grab its tail in the fast-running rapids

> and try and steer it towards the trees. He got hooked up in a clump of ti-trees with the dog in its mouth, and when that happened I stomped on its tail and worked up towards his back legs, stomping as hard as I could.

During the struggle the crocodile let go of the dog but then grabbed it again. Finally, as Thomas continued to jump on the animal's hindquarters, it let the dog go and swam towards the mouth of the river.

Thomas said he expected to lose his hand or at least sustain serious bites, but luckily he came out of the ordeal injury-free. JD wasn't so lucky. The dog suffered severe wounds to its neck, back and rump, which required 63 stitches and the insertion of three drains to clean the wounds.

Thomas said he acted instinctively, but didn't think he could save his dog. 'I didn't think I'd see my dog again, but I didn't think my own life was in immediate danger because I was behind the crocodile and he would have had to turn around to get me. But if we'd been in open water, he would have taken me for sure.'

Thomas believed the crocodile had watched him swimming with his dog on previous occasions and was waiting patiently in the water before going in for the kill. Although Thomas 'wouldn't recommend' anyone else trying his Crocodile Dundee-style rescue, he didn't regret his actions. 'My mate was in trouble and I went to her aid,' he said. 'That son of a bitch wasn't going to get my dog without a fight.'

* * *

Six months later, Eric Slatter wasn't so lucky, and almost lost his own life while rescuing his dog late at night in the Russell River near Babinda, south of Cairns. Thirty-three-year-old Slatter was savagely mauled about the head as he jumped in the river to save his boxer dog, which had become trapped in the current. Slatter had swum across the river and was wading back in to deep water when he saw the dog struggling in the fast-flowing current. 'I tried to drag him out to the shallows when something hit me,' he said.

Slatter thought he had been hit by a log because of the sheer force of the blow to the head, but soon realised it was a crocodile when he was rolled and pulled underwater. Slatter survived because a friend rushed into the river, grabbed him by the feet and pulled him backwards to safety. 'My mate helped me to the car because I couldn't stand up properly,' he said. 'I kept falling over. I was really scared when I got to the shore. I was crying.'

Slatter later underwent neurosurgery in Townsville to repair his fractured skull. He also suffered deep wounds to his face and neck. Doctors found fragments of his skull embedded in the wounds. Although the crocodile was not sighted during the attack, wildlife rangers estimated the crocodile was about 2.7 metres long.

The dog, Bouncer, escaped unscathed.

In August 1999, Aranus Pilka was attacked by a crocodile while standing in thigh-deep water at MacArthur Island off Cape York Peninsula. The crocodile had Pilka by the leg and was trying to 'death roll' him into deeper water when his friend, David Winkworth, ran to his aid.

Winkworth, alerted by Pilka's screams, rushed into the water, wrapped his arms around the crocodile, forcing it to release its hold. Pilka escaped with deep lacerations to his leg. Winkworth received a bravery award from the Governor-General for his heroism.

An attack that had newspaper sub-editors sharpening their pencils with glee happened in August 2000, when ship-loader operator Phil Aspinall was bitten on the buttocks while walking through mangroves on the Pine River, north of Weipa. Headlines such as 'Escape from Croc by Seat of Pants' abounded in the nation's press, creating media mirth in not only newspapers, but radio and television as well.

Aspinall took it all in his stride(s), reacting with laid-back humour worthy of Paul Hogan at his best. 'There wasn't a lot of time to see what happened,' he told a reporter after the incident. 'It was a just a snap and then gone type thing. I must have stepped on its tail and he turned around, with his head and shoulders out of the water, and gave me a nip right on the top of the pants.'

Aspinall had been 'tramping around in thick mud' with his dog Thumpa in an isolated part of the river when the attack happened, leaving him with half a dozen puncture marks and torn skin on his right buttock. He then walked 400 metres back to his dinghy, another half an hour boat trip to his vehicle, and then an hour's drive to Weipa, before he received treatment.

The laconic father of two said his wife 'took a bit of convincing' that he had been bitten on the posterior by a crocodile after his kids announced: 'Mum, Dad's got a hole in his pants, he's been bitten by a crocodile!'

And the length of the crocodile? 'Don't they say they're all about five metres when they're hanging off your arse?' he laughed. It was actually about two metres.

But the crocodile that attacked Anthony Berndt while he slept at his campsite by the North Kennedy River at Hann Crossing in Lakefield National Park was much bigger, and much more dangerous. At about 2 am on Saturday, 21 July 2001, Berndt awoke in horror with a heavy weight across his chest. It was a four-metre crocodile. Frozen with shock, Berndt realised the crocodile had him by the wrist and was dragging him from his swag towards a deep pool known as Suicide Water Hole, about 15 metres from the campsite.

Terrified, Berndt screamed for help, alerting his mate who loaded a crossbow and fired an arrow at the crocodile, hitting it in the shoulder. Although crossbows are illegal in Queensland national parks, along with other weapons (unless they are dismantled and secured), Berndt told a Brisbane newspaper that the shot saved his life. 'Paul got an arrow into him and he got off me,' he said. Berndt, a 36-year-old bricklayer's labourer from Newell

Beach near Mossman, declined to talk further about the incident.

The two men drove more than 300 kilometres from their campsite to Mossman Hospital, bypassing two ranger stations and ignoring a detour to the nearest hospital at Cooktown. Berndt was later treated for injuries to his right wrist at Cairns Base Hospital.

A Queensland wildlife officer said because the campsite was near a deep waterhole where large crocodiles were common, it was obvious there was an element of danger, but he had never heard of one crawling across a sleeping man's chest. 'This is not typical behaviour for a crocodile,' he said.

One month after the attack, a 4.3-metre crocodile was trapped by wildlife rangers about 10 kilometres from the scene on the North Kennedy River. Queensland Parks and Wildlife Service ranger Brent Vincent said he was confident they had the crocodile that attacked Berndt. 'We are quite sure this is the crocodile because it is the dominant male in the area, which he indicated to us on the first night we spotted him by swaying high in the water to show us his size,' Vincent said. 'He weighed 700 kilograms. He was a very big animal.'

Vincent said Berndt and his friend had camped 70 metres closer to the river than they were permitted and there was a crocodile warning sign at the site. 'Those people should not have been there,' he said. 'It was quite a high tide and, in fact, if that tide had been 0.4 of a metre higher, that man would have been floating down the river.' The captured crocodile was removed from the area and released in an undisclosed location.

* * *

Having a few drinks with your mates by the river on a pleasant moonlit night is normally a lot of fun, but for 18-year-old Drewe Ramsden it almost cost him his life. The teenage plant operator and a group of eight friends were skylarking on the banks of the Barron River at about 10.30 pm in December 2004, when a crocodile grabbed him by the head as he washed his face at the water's edge. 'It just went whack. I didn't even know what hit me,' Ramsden said. 'I had my head underwater, but my mates saw the croc coming about 30 metres away and were yelling out "croc, croc".'

Fortunately for him, his friends scared off the estimated 2.5-metre crocodile by hurling bottles and rocks at the animal. 'They threw half a carton—all their grog—at it. One of my mates was probably about three metres away, throwing rocks at it.'

The attack happened downstream from Lake Placid, a suburb of Cairns barely 12 kilometres from the city centre. The lake itself is a tranquil freshwater swimming area used extensively by locals to cool off on hot summer days.

Ramsden believed he survived because the crocodile did not have a strong enough hold on his head. 'I don't think it grabbed me good enough. It pretty much used the left side of its snout and ripped the side of my jaw.' As soon as he was free, Ramsden ran to safety up the bank. 'I felt my head first. There was a puncture on the top of my head. Then I felt like a little itch on my chin. I put my hands there and my fingers fell straight into the wounds. He'd almost taken my chin off.'

Three days later a 2.6-metre crocodile was harpooned and removed by wildlife officers five kilometres downstream from where the attack occurred. A 2.15-metre animal was trapped the same night at Saltwater Creek in the city.

Global adventurer Jason Lewis almost ended his round-the-world journey in the jaws of a five-metre crocodile when the beast attacked his leaking kayak off Cooktown in March 2005. The 37-year-old Londoner was almost at the end of a 48-kilometre sea journey from Lizard Island to the Queensland mainland, as part of his quest to become the first person to circumnavigate the world without assistance from machine-operated vehicles, when the cruising crocodile closed in on his ailing craft.

Lewis paddled furiously for the nearest beach with the animal keeping pace about three metres behind him. 'I paddled as fast as I could, but the faster I paddled, the quicker the croc followed me,' he said. The frantic Briton scrambled up the beach to the relative safety of a patch of scrub, forced to leave his satellite phone and survival gear in the kayak.

Lewis watched in disbelief as the crocodile 'staked out' his craft, showing no inclination to move back into the water. Desperate to reach his phone and call for help, the stranded adventurer rushed the craft several times armed with a paddle, but each time the crocodile lunged at him, hissing aggressively. He was left with no alternative but to spend a sleepless night in the scrub without food or water as the crocodile patrolled the area around his kayak.

At daybreak, Lewis once again approached, waving the paddle in front of him. The crocodile promptly latched onto it and a hair-raising struggle ensued. Finally, Lewis was able to free the paddle and strike the crocodile over the head with it, breaking it in half in the process. Unexpectedly, the animal retreated into the water and Lewis was able to reach his phone, and a few hours later he was rescued by a sea plane and flown to Cooktown.

Lewis began his solo trip in England in 1994 and had travelled 20,000 kilometres using only paddle-and-pedal power. In October 2007, Lewis reached the River Thames and crossed his starting point, the Meridian Line at Greenwich, completing his 13-year, 74,000-kilometre epic circumnavigation of the globe.

A 'snap-happy' crocodile could be forgiven for biting a tourist on the leg after it was harassed to pose for a photograph at the Cape York resort village of Cape Tribulation. In November 2006, Belgian visitor Stefaan Vanthournout, 24, tempted fate when he spotted the two-metre animal in a creek and decided to get a close-up shot. Vanthournout, his girlfriend and four other tourists waded through shin-deep water in Masons Creek, a tributary of the Daintree River, with cameras at the ready. In spite of already breaking all the rules, including walking past two crocodile warning signs, Vanthournout then proceeded to slap the water with a stick at close quarters, trying to entice the animal to lift its body higher for the cameras.

It obliged, suddenly rearing out of the water and biting Vanthournout on the knee. The Belgian was lucky and got away with deep puncture marks that didn't require surgery. And he didn't get the photo.

Then in October 2007, Matt Martin was camping alone at Cow Bay, a pristine beach north of the Daintree River, deep in crocodile country, when he decided a sunset swim would be a good idea. It wasn't.

Martin later admitted to a journalist he was 'well into half a slab' of beer when he dived into the water—straight on top of a lurking crocodile. The startled animal reacted instantly, grabbing at Martin's face, leaving serious lacerations that later required 40 stitches.

The 35-year-old construction worker from New South Wales said the fact he was only in waist-deep water probably saved his life. 'It was like I had hit something hard like a rock, but the rock had movement . . . the next thing I'm standing up and my head was screaming "it's a croc", and I started to back-pedal fast. I thought I was dead.' Martin got away with his life because the crocodile clearly wasn't big enough to roll him into deeper water—and he just as clearly had a vast amount of luck on his side.

Despite the scare—and a face that was 'pretty messed up'—the lone traveller decided to go to bed before seeking medical treatment. He slept for seven hours. The next morning he drove to Mossman Hospital, holding a towel against his face.

After he was stitched up, Martin reflected on what the outcome of his encounter might have been. 'I started to see images of the croc . . . I saw the rib cage and left paw, the skin and the way it looked.' Martin, who had stopped over in north Queensland on his way to Darwin, said he held no grudge against the crocodile because it was only reacting against him jumping on top of its body. 'It was a bit of a back-hander, a bit of "you're in my territory". He wasn't serious, he had all the cards and he played it soft.'

Once again, the Queensland Parks and Wildlife Service issued a warning that had been repeated many times before, that 'alcohol, croc country and swimming were a dangerous mix'. Spokesman Dr Mark Read stated the obvious: 'Those things are a really bad combination and increases someone's exposure to a dangerous situation. There needs to be appropriate human behaviour in croc country and that means not swimming or wading in water where there are crocs.'

In March 2008, Cairns resident Connie Vereyen did the right thing when she took her early morning swim inside the stinger safety net at Trinity Beach. The only trouble was, a three-metre crocodile was already in the enclosure!

Varheyen, 55, was busy swimming laps at 8 am—as she had done every day for the past four years—when she came within a half metre of a 'log covered in barnacles'. When the 'log' eye-balled her, however, she instantly realised she was in trouble. 'It was scabby and I saw eyes and it spouted water at me. I thought a log is not supposed to look like that, I have to get out of here.' Verheyen said she 'walked on water' in her haste to exit the enclosure, 'fast enough to make the Olympic team'.

'To come eye-to-eye, so close, it was very frightening. I thought he was going to dive under and get me. Obviously he wasn't hungry or he would've got me there and then.' Lifesavers lowered the net enclosure to free the animal, which they believed had somehow got under the boom during the night and couldn't get out again.

Stinger nets, designed to protect swimmers from the deadly box jellyfish, have been a feature at popular north Queensland beaches for many years, but this was the first time a large crocodile had entered an enclosure.

Many other attacks have been reported over the years but cannot be substantiated through lack of witnesses or other evidence. Some would be false, the result of practical jokes, or efforts to attract media attention. And there is no doubt some attacks go unreported, through fear of ridicule or illegal activity. There is also little doubt that escapes from crocodile attacks will continue—more from luck than good judgement. Old hands on the Cape shake their heads at the foolhardy behaviour of humans in crocodile country. They have a motto: 'If you give a crocodile a chance in his own environment, he will eat you.' Wise words that should perhaps be posted on official warning signs.

PART 4:
CROC BITES

26 THE CROCODILE HATERS

The killing of crocodiles was lawful in Queensland until both the saltwater and freshwater species were protected by 1974. Before that year, the animals were shot by professionals for profit, and by others for sport—either for a trophy or simply the 'thrill of the kill'. However dubious these pursuits were, shooters—for whatever reason—were not breaking the law. But since that year, killing or harming crocodiles was declared a serious offence, punishable by fines of up to $225,000 and/or two years' imprisonment. Nevertheless, for reasons unknown—perhaps for revenge, hatred or simple-minded vandalism—crocodiles have been slaughtered and mutilated in unjustifiable acts of cruelty.

The animals have been shot, bludgeoned, decapitated, hooked and drowned in a disturbing series of incidents in north Queensland over recent years. These include a

4.2-metre male crocodile found dead from a gunshot wound in the Herbert River near Ingham in May 1999, and a 2.9-metre animal washed up on the Cairns Esplanade in February 2002. This particular crocodile died from blood poisoning caused by two 10-centimetre-long hooks embedded in its chest.

Two months later, a 1.5-metre female crocodile was killed in a bizarre attack at Edmonton, south of Cairns. The animal was found in a garden bed on a busy road. Wildlife officers said it had been killed with 'two massive blows behind the head with a sharp object'. The tail had been severed and then crudely reattached using pieces of wire.

That was followed by the discovery of a dead crocodile found in the inner-city Cairns suburb of Portsmith with its head cut off and its tail also removed. Then in quick succession two crocodile skins measuring 2.7 metres and 1.5 metres respectively were found in the city with the feet still attached. Queensland Parks and Wildlife Service senior conservation officer Dr Mark Read said the carcasses of the animals were not found, suggesting they were killed for their meat. 'This is the first time crocodiles have been found skinned in the inner city and it's quite bizarre to say the least,' Read said. 'It's a poor job of skinning so it's likely whoever did this is not a professional.'

Perhaps the greatest act of cruelty was carried out on a 1.5-metre juvenile crocodile that was first injured by a harpoon, then its jaws were bound together, and finally left to die in Trinity Inlet. Read said the crocodile's death was a continuing part of a disturbing trend. 'They left this crocodile to die a very slow and cruel death. It can't feed or drink—it's a dreadful act—to mutilate an animal, especially like that. They fated this animal to die.'

Following a spate of daily crocodile sightings in Cairns city in October 2007, two boys openly admitted to bashing a 1.8-metre animal to death with a rock. The boys, aged 12 and 14, said they killed the crocodile because it was in a drain near their home in Westcourt and they feared for the safety of local residents. 'We got a torch, a big hook and some meat and went down and got it,' they told the media.

Police and Queensland Parks and Wildlife Service officials were not impressed, however, and the two boys were ordered to attend a Youth Justice Conference to further explain their behaviour. Police later charged a 23-year-old Westcourt man over the same incident. The charges included one of animal cruelty and another of disturbing a dangerous native animal in the wild.

The incident attracted media attention from all over Australia. Public opinion was divided over the killing of the animal, with some commentators applauding the offenders for taking action in the name of safety, while others called for stern penalties.

On 29 November, in the Cairns Magistrates Court, Owen Pacellie Dorante pleaded guilty to killing the crocodile. The court heard Dorante helped the two boys haul the crocodile from the drain and then repeatedly bash its head with rocks. The boys took turns beating the animal with a metal bar. The Westcourt man was ordered to carry out 180 hours of community service and pay a $500 fine for what Magistrate

Suzette Coates called 'a very foolish [and] complete error of judgement'.

RSPCA Queensland senior inspector Michael Pecic called the punishment 'extremely lenient' and would send out a message to people that animal cruelty was not a serious issue. 'Maiming or killing a protected animal is disgusting and it's questionable if the penalty was severe enough for this sort of action,' he said. Dorante expressed remorse for the incident, saying he fully deserved the court's penalty. 'I'm very sorry. The two boys asked for help, but it's not something I would normally get involved with.'

Three weeks later, the mutilated corpse of a crocodile was discovered at Holloways Beach, an inner suburb of Cairns. The animal's head, tail, and three of its legs were missing. Authorities believed trophy hunters had slaughtered the animal.

The Queensland Parks and Wildlife Service warned that interfering with crocodiles was illegal and would not be tolerated. 'The safety of people is paramount,' a QPWS statement read, 'but any suggestion that people take the law into their own hands is highly irresponsible and extremely dangerous.'

In October 1994, the carcass of a five-metre crocodile was found in the mangroves lining a creek near Bamaga. The huge animal's head was missing, believed to have been removed with a chainsaw. Seven months later a resident of the area who reported the slaughter condemned the Department of Environment and Heritage (DEH) for its inaction over the killing. The resident said he couldn't allow his name to be used because he feared the offenders, who had escaped prosecution, would retaliate against him or his family. 'They're well known in the area as bad boys and I can't take the risk,' he said. The local man said the men were professional fishermen from the Tully region and both the police and DEH officials knew who they were, but a planned raid had stalled because of a lack of cooperation between the two departments. He said he had lived in the north of Cape York for 25 years but had never seen a crocodile mutilated in this way.

> The head had been cut off neatly and only a chainsaw could have done such a job. They must have taken it home for a trophy, so it wouldn't be hard for police to find, but nothing has happened. It's a disgrace and that's why I'm speaking out.

The resident said he observed two men and a youth in the area of Jackey Jackey Creek at the time. They were working crab pots and netting for barramundi, but he noticed neither the pots nor the nets carried identification numbers, which were required by law.

> It all looked pretty suspicious to me, so I took the registration numbers of their two vehicles and a tinnie they were using, just in case something was going on. The next day they packed up in a hurry and took off and I haven't seen them since.

He said a local guide told him of the headless crocodile that same afternoon, so he took photos of the carcass and reported the matter to police and a DEH ranger. 'That's the last I heard of it,' he said.

Sergeant Trevor Crawford, officer in charge at Bamaga, confirmed he had received the information, including the registration numbers of the dinghy and vehicles. 'Yes, I know about this incident and I passed all details on to the relevant DEH officers as I'm obliged to do,' he said.

DEH staff refused to comment on the issue but it was believed Townsville officers had been notified of the mutilation and had requested Tully police for assistance to mount a raid. That assistance was allegedly denied because senior police in Cairns were 'unhappy' with the way the DEH had handled a previous illegal operation on Cape York. A DEH source said tissue samples from the crocodile's head could have been matched to samples from the carcass and DNA tested to prove a case 'if things had gone as they should have in the first place'. The acting officer in charge of Tully Police, Graham Lohmann, said he had no personal knowledge of the incident, nor of any request for help in a raid.

But the crocodile death that caused by far the most public outrage was the killing of Old Slimy in the Daintree River in July 1990. Old Slimy, a 4.2-metre male saltwater crocodile was a landmark tourist attraction, well known for patrolling his section of the river, about 1.5 kilometres upstream from the ferry crossing and eight kilometres from Daintree township. He was fondly regarded as a 'local' by residents and river boat operators, and the subject of thousands of photographs—some of which featured on tourist brochures and postcards.

The crocodile was shot in broad daylight with a single large-calibre bullet, but there were no witnesses to the killing.

River boat operator Chris Dahlberg saw the crocodile lying on the riverbank just before it was shot in the early afternoon. He heard the gunshot and watched as birds took flight from the mangroves, but assumed pig hunters were in the area. When he saw the crocodile a short time later the animal 'was in an odd position, with its tail in the water'. Dahlberg noticed a large hole in the crocodile's side and blood coming from its mouth. 'It is quite a tragedy as he is the largest crocodile we've seen,' he said.

Underwater explorer and filmmaker Ben Cropp saw Old Slimy die. The internationally renowned marine expert was shooting documentary footage on the river and was on hand to record the animal's dying moments.

> I was actually filming him and it must have been just after the shooting, because he started to act strangely. Then I heard him growl, and he coughed up blood and tossed his head before sliding into the water. He'd been in the river for about 10 years and this was just a tragedy.

The shooting once again divided the township of Daintree, as it did when resident Beryl Wruck was killed by a crocodile in December 1985 (see Chapter 12). Hostilities resurfaced between residents who had lived in the area for two and three generations, and the new-breed entrepreneurs who brought tourism to the town. Tour operators were convinced 'old guard' locals planned and carried out the 'execution' of Old Slimy, but other residents believed itinerant 'hoons' were responsible—probably pig hunters stopping off for a bit of sport on their way further north to Cooktown.

Dean Clapp then owned the Crocodile Express river cruise and the Daintree Butterfly Farm—the scene of the Beryl Wruck tragedy five years earlier. Clapp didn't point the finger at anyone, but he believed the shooting was planned, and not a fly-by-night event.

> If it was some Rambo hoon, how did he find his way to that spot through the canefields and stumble onto a spot not far from a big, sun-basking crocodile—you'd have to be lucky. In my opinion the killing goes back to Beryl Wruck. It's the same connection.

Barney Booth didn't see it that way. Booth was born in the area and knew the river like the back of his hand. He agreed there were two camps in the town since tourism arrived. 'Locals don't mind crocs, but not as pets,' he said.

> You see, the trouble is, boat operators used to feed the crocs so they could get closer for the tourists. I don't know if they are still doing that, but if they are, they should be stopped.
>
> Local people like to go fishing, and if you're out there in a tinnie, you don't want a big croc coming up looking for a feed. They can tip a tinnie over, no trouble.
>
> You have to educate crocs to stay away from boats, and if they get too close, you have to shoot over their heads to remind them.

Booth believed the killer of Old Slimy was a shooter from out of town—what he called the 'drive-through element'. 'You can't do anything about them unless you catch them in the act,' he said. 'They even pinch the croc warning signs for souvenirs. Absolute hoons.'

Queensland National Parks and Wildlife Service officer Brent Vincent said the department had adopted a tough attitude on the killing of crocodiles, and the death of Old Slimy had resulted in a top-priority investigation. 'We're treating this very seriously,' he said. 'We are losing crocodiles on the Daintree every year. Since Beryl Wruck died, a body of people have been responsible for many deaths and we intend to get our hands on the people who are responsible for the shootings. We're out to nail them.' But that didn't happen and the killer of Old Slimy remains unknown.

27 CRAZY CROC CAPERS

Cairns is promoted internationally as the 'fun in the sun' tourism capital of Queensland, but the glossy brochures and slick advertising campaigns fail to mention the northern city is also the crocodile capital of Australia. Crocodiles inhabit the creeks and waterways that meander through and around the city, and why wouldn't they? The region is part of their natural habitat, and the city was built smack bang in the middle of it. In fact, Cairns sits on a reclaimed area of swamp, sand ridges and mangroves. Lake Street, in the central business district, is aptly named, because that is exactly what it originally was—a swampy, mosquito-infested lake.

Barely one kilometre from the city centre is a low-lying wetland area, fed by rivulets from Trinity Inlet. The area is protected from development and is part of an intricate system of waterways that include Centenary Lakes, a park popular with locals for barbeques and picnics. It is also a favourite spot for crocodiles, with a ready supply of fish, turtles and birdlife to make life easy. They've also learned they won't be shot or otherwise harmed.

In June 2007, a motorist decided to have a closer look at the lake when he spotted a random breath-testing unit up ahead. He pulled over and dived into the water, swimming haphazardly in all directions. Police shouted warnings that crocodiles inhabited the lake and that the man's life was at risk. After 10 minutes he emerged and blew 0.170—more that three times the legal limit. Police revealed later in court that the man had recently moved to Cairns from Victoria. 'He may not have had much to do with crocodiles down there,' the prosecutor told an amused court.

Crocs in the city are not big news for locals, who view the situation as entertaining and just another part of their unique city. In one two-year period, 50 of the animals were trapped in Cairns waterways and relocated to wildlife farms.

In October 2004, a 2.5-metre crocodile attracted hordes of people to the Esplanade as it made several appearances, cruising to within three metres of the shore. Incredibly, despite numerous local media reports about the animal, a 31-year-old man decided to go swimming less than 24 hours later—and promptly got stuck in the mudflats and had to be rescued by water police. The man's head was just above water on a rising tide when he was pulled free.

In late 2007, crocodile sightings in the city increased to become an almost daily occurrence, with the animals turning up in drains, creeks—and even backyards. Melissa Dayag was startled to discover a two-metre saltie sunning itself on a creek bank adjoining the backyard of her suburban Westcourt home. She said it was 'scary' because the croc was basking very close to a pedestrian walkway.

Just one week later, Stanley Leszczewicz was 'wetting a line' in Fearnley Street drain, opposite his panel-beating workshop, when he hooked the strangest catch of his life. A two-metre crocodile snatched a new lure Leszczewicz was testing, but decided he didn't like the taste, spitting it out and retreating to the opposite bank. But when the media arrived, the crocodile took advantage of the photo opportunity by lunging again at the hooked lure for the cameras. Nearby workers claimed a larger crocodile also inhabited the inner-city drain, where children often played on hot summer days.

The next day, yet another crocodile made the news, relaxing on the banks of Moodys Creek, alongside a busy street in Westcourt. And the following day, all beaches north of the city were closed when a three-metre crocodile was spotted cruising close to shore.

The croc invasion continued when, 24 hours later, a crowd gathered to watch a saltwater crocodile feast on a bloated dog carcass in a Westcourt creek. While the spectators—including several children who had been frolicking in the water—watched, the two-metre crocodile suddenly lunged onto the opposite bank and snatched a bird in its jaws, swallowing it instantly, before sliding back into the water to resume its feast on the dog.

And at Miriwinni, south of the city, a horse was attacked by a crocodile as it drank from the Russell River. Natalie

Sacchetti said her horse Whisky had his bottom lip 'ripped off' in an area of the river frequented by recreational fishing people. 'It's a beautiful waterhole, but if that had been a fisherman and not a horse, he'd be gone,' she said.

Croc encounters of a different kind are also not unknown in the city of Cairns. Taxi driver Ian Plant rescued a small crocodile from busy Mulgrave Road, 2.5 kilometres from the city centre in August 2003. The one-metre saurian was being harassed by a crowd of drunken onlookers when the cabbie pulled up at 2.30 am to investigate the disturbance. He said the animal, which he named Gnasher, put up a fierce struggle before it was captured.

Two years before that, a large crocodile was run over and killed on the road leading to Cairns Airport. The road passes over a saltwater creek and is lined with mangroves. The female 2.7-metre croc had been hit by several vehicles, and had severe injuries including a smashed pelvis and broken ribs. Queensland Parks and Wildlife senior ranger Brent Vincent said the animal may simply have been crossing the road, or it could have been lying on the bitumen for warmth during the cold night. 'This is a 75-kilogram animal and if a small car ran over it the driver would have been hard pressed to control the vehicle hitting a bump that size.' Police said they got a call at 3.50 am and 'upon arrival we found one very deceased crocodile in the middle of the road'.

Another crocodile suffered a similar fate when it was hit by a train as it crossed the railway tracks at Giru, 50 kilometres south of Townsville in April 2002. This was a big crocodile—3.4 metres in length and weighing 200 kilograms—big enough to derail the train if the driver hadn't braked when the animal was sighted down the track.

And in October 2007, Tully resident Cherie Jenkins ran over a two-metre crocodile when it unexpectedly darted under her vehicle at night. The animal died on impact.

Crane driver Chris Schumacher, or 'Shoey' to his mates, had a workplace, health and safety issue in April 2005 when he wrestled a 1.5-metre crocodile that appeared in his Cairns steel-fabricating workshop. Schumacher did a Crocodile Dundee manoeuvre, 'just like you see in the movies', to subdue the hissing animal until help arrived. 'I put a rag over its head, then we taped up its mouth and locked it in the shower until the croc handlers came and took it away,' he said.

Another invader of the workplace was a three-metre saurian nicknamed Fat Albert, which took up residence in the Cairns City Council's wastewater treatment plant for more than six years. When the crocodile was finally captured, it was discovered that Fat Albert was really Fat Alberta. She was sent off to a wildlife farm for breeding duties.

In March 2002, further north at Cooktown, local resident and keen fisherman Gordon Duncan got the shock of his life when he hauled in a crab pot he'd set the night before. There were two live crabs in the home-made pot, plus an unwelcome visitor—a dead crocodile. Somehow the two-metre croc had managed the Houdini-like feat without damaging the pot, and had eventually drowned. Duncan said he had been crabbing in the area for 58 years, but this catch was a first. 'I don't know how he got in because he hasn't broken the pot, but I've never, ever seen a crocodile in a crab pot,' he said.

An international media frenzy occurred in June 2000 when the crew of a prawn trawler reported seeing a randy crocodile trying to mate with the float of a sea plane moored off Knight Island, about 140 kilometres north of Cooktown. The witnesses put a spotlight on the plane and watched in amazement as a 'very, very big crocodile' overturned the aircraft during its amorous advances. The animal had crawled onto the float, its weight capsizing the plane.

Cooktown Coastguard officer Don Sinclair said he fielded more than 30 media calls from Australia, the United Kingdom and the United States, the day after the story broke. 'We've spoken to every state in Australia about this, the radio stations have gone crazy,' he said. 'One of the reporters asked what condition the plane was in and he was told it was rooted, but it went right over his head. They're not too bright in the cities down south.'

The plane's owner, Ted Von Nida, who had flown to the area with spare parts for a stranded trawler, said the incident was over 'in 30 seconds'. He was asleep on the deck of a nearby yacht when he was awakened by a loud splash and the plane tipped backwards, tail down, nose high, before tipping over.

We'd seen a four-metre crocodile sunbaking on the beach that afternoon, but I don't know what caused the aircraft to go over. I can only assume something very large came up out of the water on to the float. Whether it was the crocodile or a very large fish we'll never know.

Cooktown locals kept themselves amused with the story for several days. Opinion was split over whether the crocodile had loving on its mind or was attacking the aircraft in defence of its territory. Bob Harvey, who was in charge of the Coastguard operation when the incident happened, said three witnesses swore the crocodile was on a lovemaking mission and the story was not made up. 'It's a pretty amazing story but it's absolutely true,' he said. 'There's no shortage of crocodiles up here but it's the first time I've ever come across one trying to breed with a sea plane. It's quite a serious thing but everyone needs to stop laughing long enough to do something about it [the crocodile].'

Further south in Townsville, a five-metre crocodile was successful in one of the most unusual court cases the city has ever seen. The crocodile, named Rin Tin Tin after the celebrity canine of 1960s television fame, won the right to remain the star attraction at Magnetic Island's Picnic Bay Backpackers Resort. The Queensland Parks and Wildlife Service had refused the resort's owner, Bill Carnell, permission to keep the crocodile on the premises, despite the fact he had complied with all the official conditions—including the construction of an $84,000 enclosure (complete with a bulletproof window to allow Rin Tin Tin to enjoy human antics in the adjacent nightclub).

In October 2000, Magistrate Laurie Verra ruled the resort was a suitable home for the huge reptile and that Carnell had ensured the enclosure met the requirements of the department. At a previous court appearance, Carnell told journalists there were already 60,000 crocodiles in captivity for 'steak and handbag' purposes, but he was being prevented from keeping one alive. 'I go and put just one crocodile in a resort and it's unthinkable,' he said.

Crocodiles have a habit of attracting worldwide attention and Madeline Tabone's wedding was no exception. Madeline, whose father Mick owned Innisfail's Johnstone River Crocodile Farm, wanted a wedding with a difference, so she nominated a two-metre croc named Little Girl to be her flower girl.

Posing with a live saltwater crocodile for her wedding photos didn't faze Madeline, who'd spent her entire life in the company of the animals. 'I grew up with Little Girl and the other crocs on the farm and I've never been afraid of them,' Madeline said. 'Little Girl is part of the family—sort of like my sister.'

But the ceremony was not without its unexpected excitement. Soon after Madeline exchanged wedding vows with fiancé Maurice Cetinic, Little Girl decided she was fed up with holding a bouquet of flowers in her jaws, so she promptly shook it to pieces, causing a little unrest among the guests. Although the groom remained calm, he admitted later he had worked out an escape plan in the event of an emergency. 'It was a bit of a worry,' he said. 'I was ready to leap the fence if things went wrong. What I hadn't worked out was how I would jump it carrying Madeline.'

Back in the early 1990s, Tony Jones led a double life that could only be called extraordinary. By day, 36-year-old Jones was a crocodile handler in a wildlife park near Cairns, and by night he was entertaining nightclub crowds as a drag queen. Mild-mannered Jones trained saltwater crocodiles up to five metres in length with confidence and courage in front of awestruck crowds, using only an ordinary plastic garden rake to control the huge beasts. But when the sun went down, the bush gear was replaced with elaborate gowns as he was transformed into the northern city's best-known female impersonator.

Jones said the success of the Australian movie, *Priscilla, Queen of the Desert*, had made his Las Vegas-style cabaret shows increasingly popular. '*Priscilla* brought flamboyant drag queen acts back into fashion, and people are enjoying the sheer spectacle of the costumes.' He said the crocodile show and his after-midnight spectaculars were just different parts of the same professions. 'You have to entertain people and I do that in both my roles.' Jones started female impersonating in Brisbane during the heady nightclub scene of the late 1970s, while working by day as a journalist.

'I gave up journalism after two years to become a full-time performer.'

His knowledge of crocodile behaviour and safety procedures was highly regarded in the industry. 'Crocodiles are magnificent but dangerous animals, and just like driving a car, you can get into trouble if you don't go by the rules.' One of his closest calls came when a five-metre crocodile named Sarge cornered him in a pen, forcing him to hastily scale a concrete wall to escape. 'It's a calculated part of the job, so you know you'll get a scare from time to time.'

Jones's night shows included song-and-dance routines, with an emphasis on custom-designed gowns, one of which, powered by electric motors that give an illusion of the outer dress gradually being replaced by another, cost $10,000 to make. Jones has been featured as the 'Croc and Frock Man' in several American magazines.

The biggest crocodile escape in the world occurred at Mission Beach in February 1991 when more than 50 of the animals staged a mass breakout as floodwaters swept through their enclosure at a wildlife park. Frantic staff and 10 trained crocodile hunters mobilised in an effort to round up the scattered reptiles, which measured up to nearly three metres long, as they spread out into adjoining wetlands and urban areas of the resort town. After a three-week 'search and capture' operation, most of the crocodiles had been rounded up, but some had made good their escape and remain on the 'wanted' list.

* * *

In July 1994, one large crocodile was the subject of an official raid on a remote Cape York property following a tip-off that the animal was being kept illegally and mistreated, possibly with a knife. The raid was carried out by environmental rangers from Cairns, Weipa-based police, and Queensland Boating and Fisheries officers. The property, at Shelburne Bay, near the tip of Cape York, is 2000 kilometres from Cairns. The dawn commando-type operation was in response to an anonymous caller who reported seeing a man with a knife harassing a crocodile inside a shed on the property.

When the raiding party stormed the property they certainly found the crocodile. The only trouble was, it was a wooden sculpture, the work of professional carver and well-known Cape York identity, Roger Spencer.

Red-faced officials attempted to patch up the botched raid with a hasty spin-doctored explanation. The Department of Environment and Heritage regional director Greg Wellard justified the raid by saying the week-long trip to the Cape was a 'familiarisation' exercise that had already been planned when the tip-off was received. 'We wouldn't normally rush 2000 kilometres just to look at a crocodile, but we are very interested in what people in isolated areas might see,' he said. 'We take any reports seriously of things that might be happening that are illegal.' Wellard concluded that the three-metre wooden crocodile was so lifelike that anybody could be fooled into thinking it was the real thing. 'My understanding is that Mr Spencer is a wood carver of some accomplishment with enormous attention to detail so it was understandable how the mistake happened.'

A police spokesman said a separate tip-off had been received that drugs were being used on the Spencer property and the police involvement in the raid was carried out with a warrant under the Drugs Misuse Act. No drugs were found.

In August 1990, Cape York safari guide Brian Strike wanted to prove that the Queensland Government's crocodile removal plan had almost eliminated the big salties from the Daintree River, thus taking away a tourist drawcard from the area. So Strike decided to attract the most attention possible—by swimming across the notoriously dangerous river, the same one where Beryl Wruck was attacked and eaten by a crocodile in 1985. Strike, who operated daily 'croc spotting' boat trips along the river, resented the fact that the area's big crocodiles were being taken from their natural habitat and sold to crocodile farms. 'These creatures are part of our heritage and they are not being protected by the very people who are supposed to do this,' he said.

Strike backed up his stand by entering the river at the Daintree ferry crossing—which links Daintree with Cape Tribulation—at 6 pm, a time when crocodiles are at their most active. 'I am not a good swimmer and I'm not in the best shape,' he said. 'My wife thinks I'm crazy, but if this will make people sit and listen, it's worth it.' But 'Strikie', as he was known, made the 350-metre crossing in one piece, gaining a fleeting moment of international fame in the process.

Renowned underwater filmmaker and marine expert Ben Cropp said, although Strike's action was foolish, it was a calculated risk that was unlikely to result in a crocodile attack. 'There are some big crocs left in the river but Mr Strike was gambling on them not being in that part of the river because they are territorial,' Cropp said. 'But what people tend to forget is that there are a lot of whaler sharks in the Daintree that will attack a man.'

Strike had luck on his side, however. Some time after his famous swim, a crocodile attacked the ferry's cable during a night-time crossing. Ferry operator Phil Smith said the animal had the cable in its jaws and was trying to 'kill it' as the ferry headed for the northern bank. 'The scary thing is that I have to tie the ferry up on the south side of the river and row across to the north side to get home,' he said. 'I've been rowing quite a bit faster lately.'

One small crocodile turned up a long way from home when water police raided a cruise boat in Nelson Bay, near Newcastle, New South Wales, on New Year's Day 1999. As well as a cache of handguns and assault rifles, a grenade and a machine gun, the water cops located a one-metre crocodile in a shower recess. Authorities said a 55-year-old man had 'stolen' the juvenile croc from Lakefield National Park and had been boasting about his exploits in a local pub. The crocodile was flown back to north Queensland and returned to its original habitat.

But the luckiest crocodile of them all is Goliath, a four-metre monster that resides in absolute comfort atop Cairns' luxury waterfront resort, the Reef Hotel Casino. Goliath is the star attraction at the Rainforest Dome, a wildlife sanctuary with views across the city and Trinity Inlet.

Goliath shares his five-star penthouse accommodation with 100 other native animals and birds, but has his own purpose-built enclosure, which contains a 30,000-litre pond, a wide variety of vegetation, and a special window so he can keep an eye on the spectators.

It's a crocodile crazy world in north Queensland and born-and-bred locals wouldn't have it any other way.

28 HOW BIG IS BIG?

Bob Plant shot crocodiles for 30 years and has a stock response to the many stories of giant crocodiles stalking the rivers of Cape York Peninsula in modern times. He says claims of animals reaching '20 feet' or more exist only in the realms of fantasy or falsehood, and he'll back up his statement with his hip pocket.

'I've got a thousand dollars in my pocket for anyone who can prove to me they've measured a 20-foot crocodile,' the legendary shooter said.

> They're not out there and they never were, no way in the world. Most big crocs are 14 to 15 feet, very few over that. They look bigger in photos, but they're not. Anyone who talks 20-foot, 24-foot, to me, is bullshittin'. Go and put your head in the mud, mate, you're tellin' lies, you haven't seen such a croc!

Bold words, but they come from a tough bushman who knows the Cape like his own backyard, and few would question his judgement. Plant says the biggest crocodile he has ever seen was one his father, Bob Plant Snr, shot in the Staaten River, estimated to have been '16 feet' in length.

> He shot it on one of his pre-war expeditions, just on dark. We couldn't accurately measure it because we didn't have a tape. It might have measured 17 foot, but I wouldn't bet on it. The bloody thing had moss growing on its back! I've got his head down in the shed.

The question of size has always dominated the subject of the Australian saltwater crocodile, and opinions vary widely. Reports of the fabled '20-footers', or bigger, are common in the folklore of the past 100 years, and continue to provoke fierce debate between experts and laymen alike. There is ample fossilised proof and other scientific evidence that so-called 'monster' or 'super' crocodiles roamed the earth in the ancient past, such as the 12-metre saurian that inhabited what is now the Sahara Desert region, and there is a strong case that crocodiles have attained 20-metre and over sizes in the Indo–Pacific region up until fairly recent times.

But in tropical north Queensland, the question of whether such super-sized animals existed in the 20th century (and perhaps still do) remains perhaps a question of trust and individual belief. Prior to the turn of that century several reports of giant crocodiles exist, but there is no real proof to back up such claims.

In 1860, a 10-metre crocodile was reportedly shot on the banks of the Mossman River, but no material evidence of this has ever been presented. Then in 1884, publican Jack O'Brien is believed to have shot a 10-metre crocodile from the verandah of the Leichhardt Hotel, situated on the banks of the Pioneer River, which runs through Mackay. The crocodile, dubbed the 'Mackay Monster', was supposedly hidden behind a canvas cover where people paid to view it, before the skin was displayed on a pub wall. The skin later mysteriously disappeared, according to the story. In 2000, a photograph of a large crocodile, purported to be the Monster, was found by a council worker at the Mackay dump, but the size of the animal cannot be accurately determined. Also in the 1880s, a 10-metre crocodile was reported to have been shot in the Russell River, just south of Cairns.

Reports of six-metre-plus crocodiles being shot by hunters on Cape York Peninsula include a 7.5-metre animal supposedly killed in the 1960s on the Annie River in Princess Charlotte Bay, and another one of the same size in a tributary of the Staaten River. Percy Trezise, a well-known pilot, artist and author who was highly respected internationally for his discovery and study of Aboriginal rock art, had no doubt he sighted several 'super' crocodiles during his many flights across Cape York Peninsula. On one charter trip in 1977, while flying a group of tourists who 'wanted to see crocodiles' he saw an animal he was certain was around 10 metres in length. Trezise recounted the experience.

> I was flying low over an estuarine area, with the tide out, and I came around a corner at 100 feet, and there was the

> crocodile of all crocodiles. It looked as if you couldn't reach across his back with spread arms. In my opinion he was more than 30 feet long. I never told anybody the location, because if I did there'd be some mad bastard out there with a gun.

Trezise, who died in 2005, was an early campaigner for the protection of crocodiles. He said big crocs were common back in the 1950s.

> In the late '50s I was flying for the Aerial Ambulance and up along the western coast, north of Weipa, I saw this big log with a fairly large crocodile nearby. When I circled the log I saw its feet and realised that it, too, was a crocodile. I reckon it was 24 feet long. A few years later a shooter named Colin Gostelow shot a 24-foot croc in the same area.

Rene Henri, founder of the Australian Crocodile Shooters' Club, described his first encounter with a crocodile during a late 1940s trip to Cooktown. With a group of sportsmen friends 'escaping the Victorian weather', he was in a rowing boat on the Endeavour River when their guide beckoned them to be silent. 'We of course did not believe that a crocodile could be so near a town but, around the bend on a sand bank, an 18-footer suddenly awakened by the noise made a dash for the water and vanished. We were stunned.'

The next day the party was invited back to the river to view the crocodile, which had been killed overnight by an Aboriginal police tracker. 'It was my first meeting with a crocodile. An 18-foot beast is impressive. It looked like a pre-historic monster. To touch it for the first time gives you the creeps.' On one of his later expeditions, Henri records that he shot and measured a '20-footer'.

The largest crocodile that Lloyd Grigg shot was '16 foot 3 inches' but he said he saw a '25-footer' in a river running into Princess Charlotte Bay. 'We were 50 yards away in the boat,' Grigg said. 'His slide mark was 5 foot 6 inches wide, and I only ever saw him once.'

Veteran crocodile shooter Jack Sweeney said 'about 18 feet' was the biggest crocodile he has encountered, but he didn't go looking for them as 'the big fellas were more trouble than they were worth' due to the age and poor quality of their skins.

Louie Komsic said he shot a monstrous '19 foot 10 inch' crocodile in a creek off the Jardine River. The first night he spotted the crocodile he couldn't get close enough to shoot. The next night, at the same spot, Komsic waded waist-deep in the creek until he saw the crocodile watching him. 'I walked towards him, he go away, then he comes back, like we're see-sawing. I kept after him, not firing the gun. Then he went crazy, what I was waiting for, and comes fast at me and I shoot him.'

The next day Komsic returned to skin the animal. 'He was huge, I measured him, but very difficult to skin because of his size. The shallow water helped me turn him around. I couldn't lift his head, so it had to stay behind. He was fat like a 44-gallon drum.' Unfortunately, Komsic didn't have a camera, so the animal was not photographed. 'I've seen a crocodile in the Archer River that could have been bigger,

20 foot or so, maybe a bit more, maybe a bit less, but it would be a rare one,' he said. 'A big crocodile like that would be like a 10 foot man! Could be there, but not many 10 foot men in the world. One or two, if any!'

George Craig has shot and trapped many big crocodiles as a hunter across the top of Australia and in Papua New Guinea, so he knows a bit about size. His star attraction at Marineland Melanesia on Green Island is Cassius, a moody croc with part of his tale missing. Cassius measures 5.3 metres, but Craig insists he is a 'true 18-footer' if his incomplete tail is taken into account.

'There was a big man-eater I was after in New Guinea, but I couldn't catch him,' Craig said.

> He was eventually caught in 1974 after we had set up on Green Island. He got himself tangled in a barra net and drowned—a lot of the big old crocs get caught that way. That bloke apparently measured 20 feet 4 inches, the biggest one I know of, a real monster. I have heard of one 20 feet 9 inches, but it hasn't been authenticated. I have yet to see a legendary 25-footer, and I don't believe one that size ever existed in modern times.

Craig agrees with Bob Plant's assertion that there are no six-metre crocodiles on Cape York Peninsula. 'I've never seen a 20-footer so I'll pay that. You see a 15 or 16 foot croc up on a bank, that's a hell of a big reptile, and you'd swear it was 20 foot. But when you put the tape on him, that's another matter.'

Rob Bredl, known as the 'Barefoot Bushman' at his family-owned wildlife park at Airlie Beach, also knows a thing or two about crocodiles and the size factor. His father Joe started Queensland's first commercial crocodile farm at Edward River (now Pormpuraaw) on Cape York, and Rob grew up hunting and capturing 'a few hundred' of the creatures.

In his book *The Real Crocodile*, Bredl states:

> There is no evidence (or I have not been able to find any), not even a photograph, of any crocodile of over 6 metres long (20').
>
> According to my calculations a 6 metre crocodile's head would be 80 centimetres long with its largest tooth being almost as thick as the top of a Coca Cola can and about 20 centimetres long . . . The crocodile would most likely weigh around three tonnes . . . A fair lump of a lizard at 10 metres would have to weigh between seven and 10 tonnes with teeth as thick as a man's arm.

Tom Cole, the legendary crocodile shooter and author of the best-selling autobiographical book *Hell West and Crooked*, was a well-known sceptic of the 'monster croc' claims. Cole, who hunted crocodiles in the Northern Territory, Cape York Peninsula and New Guinea, was a highly respected authority on the saltwater species until his death in 1995. He had this to say on the subject of size:

> A lot of nonsense has been written, and much more talked about, the size to which they are supposed to grow, 30 and 40 feet being freely mentioned. This I find hard to believe. I first started hunting crocodiles professionally in 1935 and

> have personally shot several thousand. I have been deeply involved in importing and exporting skins in large quantities. I introduced commercial hunting to New Guinea and over a long period of time I have handled in the vicinity of 50,000 skins.
>
> The largest crocodile I ever shot myself was on the Victoria River in the Northern Territory, which measured 18 feet 9 inches. I shot one in the Kikori Delta of Papua, which went 18 feet 6 inches. Another, which lived in the Gogol River, until it met me, was 18 feet 3 inches.
>
> The largest skin I have ever seen was from Borneo. A portion of its tail was missing, but I believe that had it been complete it might have made 20 feet.
>
> I think it's reasonable to assume that of 50,000 skins, if crocodiles had generally grown much longer than 20 feet I would have seen at least one.

Former crocodile shooter and skin dealer Bryan Peach purchased a skin '19 foot' long from Innisfail shooter Jack King, who shot the animal in Liverpool Creek, south of the sugar town. Retired federal politician Warren Entsch, who trapped crocodiles in the wild during the 1980s, is a firm debunker of the 'monster' crocodile claims.

> We'd get reports from the public about these huge crocs out there, but when we caught them they were significantly smaller. You could put people on a lie detector and they'd swear they saw crocodiles over 20 feet long, but without exception, they were nowhere near that size. It wasn't that people were lying, it was just that crocodiles are so

awe-inspiring, they tend to look much bigger than they really are.

But there is another event that adds even more controversy to the question of crocodile size—are there huge 'monster crocs' on Cape York or aren't there?

When the husband-and-wife crocodile shooting team of Ron and Krys Pawlowski announced that in 1957 Krys had killed an 8-metre-plus giant on the Norman River, the news created a sensation—even more so when it became known that the attractive, Polish-born adventurer had killed the beast with a single shot. Thus, she earned herself the media nickname 'One Shot Krys' (see Chapter 7).

Considering the size—8.63 metres—is in the fabled 'monster croc' category, there was considerable scepticism among the shooters of the day, some of whom scoffed at the claim. And there was a problem. The Pawlowskis could not produce any evidence of the kill. There was no head, and there were no photographs. No shooter would miss the opportunity to prove such a one-in-a-million feat was genuine, was the prevailing opinion among the hard-heads on the Cape. But the Pawlowskis stuck to their story, ignoring the criticism with stoic silence, firm in the knowledge that what they said had happened was the truth.

In July 2007, exactly 50 years after the event, Ron Pawlowski responded with dignified calm to suggestions that some of his contemporaries still refused to believe the story. 'It's jealousy, they wanted to see it first, but we did,' he said. 'It doesn't matter to me what people believe. I'm saying what happened.' And this is what Ron Pawlowski said happened.

> We spotted this very large crocodile a good half-mile distant, on the bank at low tide. We thought it might be a croc we'd seen before, that we estimated at 27 to 30 feet. We called him Pop because we reckoned he was the granddaddy of them all.
>
> I told Krys he was too big to lift and to skin, and too big to sell, but we tied up the boat and walked through the mangroves, keeping low. Krys crept closer, until she was 25 metres away, still covered by the mangroves. Then 'bang!' she shot him through the ear with a silver-tipped expanding bullet that turned his giant's brain into mush.
>
> It was a terribly sad occasion. We had killed a king.

The Pawlowskis used a depth-sounding stick to measure the animal and repeated the process three times. They were satisfied with the accuracy of their measurement. It was 28 feet 4 inches. Ron Pawlowski said he had three Kodachrome transparency frames left in his camera, which he used to photograph the crocodile.

They were faced with a dilemma. The crocodile could not be moved 'an inch' by hand, and they had no lifting equipment on their boat for such a task. Also, there was no machinery at Karumba or Normanton capable of hauling the beast into deeper water and towing it elsewhere, plus the cost of such an operation was beyond their means at the time. And there was another problem. A skin of that magnitude could not be preserved by Australian tanneries of the day, and would have to be sent to Singapore, which they could not afford to do. So the massive carcass—the biggest in the world—was left where it was shot, on the muddy bank of the river. A huge carcass was later seen drifting along the river towards the sea by the crew of a scientific vessel studying prawn movements in the Gulf of Carpentaria.

Ron Pawlowski's three photographs were processed in Melbourne, and he said he was 'exceedingly satisfied' with their quality. He subsequently filed them with the rest of his photographic material.

In 1960, the Pawlowskis received an offer of one thousand dollars from the American Museum of Natural History for a crocodile skeleton of monstrous size, but they rejected the offer as not worth the trouble, even if the remains could be located, which was extremely doubtful. 'That amount wouldn't even pay for the cost of recovering the skeleton, so we weren't interested,' Ron Pawlowski said.

Then in 1968, when the Pawlowskis were forced from their Karumba leasehold by the state government, he destroyed much of his research material. It was an act born of frustration, disappointment and anger. Unfortunately, two of the transparencies of the giant crocodile were mistakenly destroyed. 'At the time it did not matter, I did not care,' he said. 'Nobody was too interested in crocodiles in those days.' But he later discovered the remaining transparency, plus a negative, were with his London agent, and both were returned at his request.

In December 1970, Ron Pawlowski received a letter from the Australian Museum with a copy of a letter from a scientific organisation in Thailand addressed to the British Museum of Natural History requesting a photograph of an exceptionally large crocodile. The British Museum contacted the Australian Museum, who then passed on the request to the Pawlowskis.

> I mailed the transparency, and the negative, together with some other photographs to an address in Bangkok, but I heard no more from them. I wrote again but received no reply. I realised the photographs were lost. In those years I had lost so much, including my health, that the loss of the photographs—although irreplaceable—faded into insignificance.

In 1978, the *Guinness Book of Records* stated: 'In July, 1957, a length of 28ft 4ins was reported for an estuarine crocodile shot by Mrs Kris [sic] Pawlowski on the MacArthur Bank of the Norman River, north-western Queensland.'

The year before, the London publication *Animal Facts and Feats* had an entry under the heading: 'The greatest authentic measurement recorded for an estuarine crocodile is 8.63 metres.' The entry read:

> In normal circumstances this measurement would be rejected because nothing of this monstrous saurian was preserved, although a photographic record existed until 1968 [sic]. However, as Mrs Pawlowski's husband Ron is one of the world's leading authorities on this species, and farmed the estuarine crocodile at Karumba, this record must be regarded as one with a high probability of accuracy.

Although no material evidence exists to prove without doubt the Pawlowskis' claim, it is difficult to imagine Ron, a man with such impeccable credentials in the fields of crocodile hunting and scientific research, and a pioneer in the protection of the species, would continue with a fabrication allegedly forged 50 years ago with his now deceased wife.

A full-sized replica of the crocodile stands outside the Carpentaria Shire Council building in Normanton. To stand beside it is to fully realise the enormity of such a beast and to consider the possibility that another—or others—of similar magnitude could exist in the many remote and inaccessible wilderness areas of Cape York today.

Ron Pawlowski is adamant his claim is genuine. Some believe him, some don't, but many observers—even among the sceptics—concede it is *possible.* The question of how big is big, therefore, cannot be answered.

29 TO CULL OR NOT TO CULL

Crocodiles have fought back since they were protected in 1974, after having been almost wiped out by widespread shooting. Now, however, saltwater crocodiles have rebounded in numbers that some observers say are out of control, encroaching on towns and cities, and posing a serious threat to humans.

Number estimates vary widely, depending on whoever is quoting them and the method of assessment used. A recent study by the Northern Territory's Charles Darwin University suggests the saltwater crocodile population in the Northern Territory alone stands at about 75,000. In Queensland, the figure most quoted is around 30,000, with Western Australia apparently having about the same population. But these numbers are little more than guesswork, and the true number of crocodiles in the wild is unknown.

There is no doubt, however, that the dangerous saurians are on the increase. Since shooting stopped, these animals continued to reproduce in their environment with no predators to keep their numbers down, and they are becoming bolder in their behaviour. Urban environments hold no fear for them as they increasingly seek out new territory. It is a fact that all coastal cities and towns in northern Australia now have a crocodile problem.

It is estimated that up to 400 crocodiles are removed annually by wildlife rangers from Darwin Harbour. All animals trapped in populated areas are sold to crocodile farms, regardless of size. None are returned to the wild.

In Queensland, crocodiles roam up and down the tropical coast and are regularly seen in populated areas from Mackay to Cooktown. In particular, the animals are increasingly located in and around the waterways of Cairns. These animals are trapped and sold to zoos or crocodile farms. The practice of relocating them to isolated areas of Cape York was abandoned and is no longer carried out by the Queensland Parks and Wildlife Service. Saltwater crocodiles have a nasty habit of returning to their original territory.

In recent years there have been several attacks on humans within Cairns city boundaries, with near fatal consequences. Many people say it is only a matter of time before somebody dies. Former Cairns Mayor Kevin Byrne is one of them. He said the animals must be removed from the city whenever they appear as 'crocodiles and humans can't live together' without the risk of a tragedy. Byrne said a number of council officers were specially trained to remove crocodiles and assist wildlife rangers when required. He said the idea of crocodiles in a modern city might be amusing to some people, but it was a serious issue that had to be dealt with in Australia's tropical north. 'There is no doubt a novelty value for people in Melbourne and Sydney to read about crocodiles running around Cairns, but it's not funny to us, and crocodiles are not welcome in our city.' Byrne said if all efforts to trap dangerous crocodiles failed, then as a last resort they should be shot. 'Yes, it's true somebody could be killed, and I don't want that to happen in Cairns. If a crocodile can't be caught and removed, then drastic action has to be taken.'

The debate for and against crocodile culling has raged for over a decade and the issue remains unresolved in both the Northern Territory and Queensland. While the Northern Territory allows the harvesting of 600 crocodiles annually for their skins and other purposes, safari—or 'trophy'—hunting remains illegal. In October 2005, the federal government rejected calls from the Northern Territory to introduce the practice.

Federal Minister for the Environment and Heritage, Senator Ian Campbell, said he had considered the proposal 'very carefully' and decided to approve the Northern Territory's overall management plan—but to reject the safari hunting component. In its submission, the Northern Territory Government had asked that trophy hunters be allowed to legally shoot 25 of the 600 crocodiles already culled each year. 'I do not believe that safari hunting of crocodiles is consistent with a modern-day approach to animal welfare and responsible management,' Campbell said publicly.

It was later revealed, however, that Campbell had seriously considered approving the safari plan, but was influenced against the option by the late Steve Irwin. Irwin, known internationally as television's 'Crocodile Hunter', was an outspoken opponent of safari hunting and had lobbied the federal government to knock back any form of culling. Irwin wrote to Campbell and then took him on a tour of Cape York Peninsula's crocodile country, when it's believed the minister was converted to the celebrity conservationist's cause.

Warren Entsch, who was then the federal member for Leichhardt—a vast electorate that covers Cape York and Torres Strait—said his government was 'stupid' not to allow the safari plan. Entsch, a former Cape York cattle man and part owner of a Northern Territory crocodile farm, said he approached Campbell several times and tried to persuade him to ratify the proposal.

> I put a submission in that we should allow the requested 25 crocodiles be taken by trophy hunters as it was a valid plan that made sense, but when Steve Irwin took Campbell on a private trip to Cape York that was the end of it—his mind was made up. I disagreed with Campbell's decision, but he was blinded by the glitz and glamour of the occasion.
>
> I told Campbell that some of those 600 crocodiles shot each year in the Northern Territory are too big for commercial use, so they are left to rot in the wild. Trophy hunters would pay big money for the animals. I urged the Northern Territory to put another plan in.

Entsch, who trapped and removed problem crocodiles from cities and towns in the 1980s, said the Queensland Government had consistently refused to lobby for a safari hunting program and did not allow the harvesting of crocodile eggs from the wild, a practice that had been in place in the Northern Territory for many years. 'Crocodiles have increased dramatically in north Queensland but to manage the numbers you have to have a proper management plan like the Northern Territory. This government doesn't have one.'

In Queensland, there is growing support for a shooting industry that would not only keep numbers down, but provide financial benefits for Cape York towns and Aboriginal communities. Calls to allow wealthy hunters the opportunity to 'bag' saltwater crocodiles for a hefty fee continue to gain momentum, but the government refuses to budge on its strict protection policy, emphasising the fact that the estuarine crocodile is listed as a vulnerable species in the state.

Instead, a conservation plan released in March 2007 included a proposal to discourage swimmers from entering the water in crocodile territory by imposing fines of up to $7500.

Then Environment Minister Lindy Nelson-Carr rejected fears that crocodile numbers were out of control, suggesting instead that the numbers of people moving around in crocodile habitats had increased, therefore crocodiles are *seen* more often, but there are not more of them. 'In developing this plan, the Environment Protection Agency aimed to get the balance right between public safety, sustainable commercial use of saltwater crocodiles and protecting these ancient, vulnerable animals in the wild,' she said.

But outspoken politician Bob Katter, the member for Kennedy, called the plan out of touch with reality and a backward step in protecting people from crocodile attacks in Queensland. 'Instead of removing crocs, they're going to remove human beings,' he said. Katter believes controlled culling should be introduced and a bounty paid on the animals, with firearms available to people in crocodile country to use for their own protection.

> Surely people have the right to protect their kids from a dangerous predatory animal. Action needs to be taken to cull crocodiles and push them out of settled areas. Shoot the bastards. The people who tell us we can't shoot them would die of fright if they saw one.

Queensland National Party Senator Ian Macdonald agreed the plan favoured animals over humans. 'I'm a great conservationist,' he said, 'but when it comes to people's lives as opposed to an explosion in crocodile population then I will always pick people's lives. There will be a tragedy.'

Long-time proponent of crocodile hunting expeditions, Cape York pastoralist Graham Elmes, is adamant the idea should be put into practice. Elmes said an American millionaire had offered $100,000 a few years ago to stalk and shoot a 'monster croc' in the wild. 'Big-game hunters would pay that kind of money for a trophy and some of that money could go back into crocodile research. It's a good idea and should be looked at seriously.'

Elmes said there should be 'zero tolerance' of crocodiles that threaten human habitation and made it plain that Cooktown residents and station owners took the matter into their own hands when necessary. 'What they've been doing is handling the situation in their own practical and commonsense manner,' he said. 'You can work out for yourself what that means.' Elmes said Aboriginal owners of the land had traditionally managed crocodile numbers by monitoring their breeding patterns and selectively removing eggs and nests in certain areas.

> They had boundaries where they allowed crocodiles to breed, but in other places where they didn't want them they made sure the nests didn't survive. They were managing crocodile numbers in their country through centuries of tradition.
>
> Modern management methods are a joke, they don't have a clue. The information that is fed to the public is diabolical, but nobody listens to the people who really know what goes on.

Cook Shire Mayor Bob Sullivan shares that opinion. He said the issue of culling and hunting safaris is 'extremely emotive' but he is in favour of a strictly controlled permit system that would benefit the economy of Cape York. 'It makes sense and could be organised and operated responsibly in consultation with the community, including indigenous land owners,' he said. Sullivan said it was difficult to get the idea promoted in a positive light because governments and bureaucrats in southern cities did not understand how things worked 'on the ground' in Cape York.

> It's hard to get the message across because they don't understand us up here and how we think. There are two totally different perspectives—how they see us and how we really are.
>
> The quality of public servants is diminishing because of the internet and modern technology. They can sit at their desk and keyboards and think they know everything. Well, they don't. They need to get up here and walk around and see what it's really like.

Sullivan said the trend to restrict human activity in Cape York in favour of 'locked up' national parks was a backward step in developing Cape York Peninsula.

> It's bloody bullshit. Eco-tourism is not the only industry that can exist and thrive up here. Crocodile shooting safaris are a great opportunity for economic development in this part of the world.
>
> We don't want cowboys out there slaughtering crocs, but selected, professional guides to run things. We're not environmental vandals up here, but we're tarred with that brush. Legislation governs us—they think we can't govern ourselves.

Sullivan pointed out the financial success the marlin fishing industry brought to Cairns in the 1950s and '60s. 'Marlin fishing put Cairns on the world map and it didn't wipe out the species. Crocodile hunting can do the same for Cooktown. Big-game hunters will pay a fortune to take home a crocodile trophy to hang on the wall. There's nothing wrong with that.'

Sullivan said the government's failed crocodile relocation program proved that the big animals always returned to their original home and there were now too many close to Cooktown. 'They are in the Endeavour River and that's too close to us. It's dangerous.'

But Queensland Parks and Wildlife Service senior conservation officer, Dr Mark Read, said the incidence of saltwater crocodiles attacking humans was very low, and the department's proactive 'crocwise' education program was the key to safe behaviour in crocodile country. 'Culling only lures people into unsafe and complacent behaviours, as it is impossible and undesirable to remove all crocodiles from the environment,' he said.

Read said warning signs placed near waterways in crocodile territory ensured people knew of the dangers and how to stay safe. 'Unfortunately most crocodile attacks occur in situations where crocodiles have learnt to associate food, such as fish scraps, with humans, or where people have underestimated the risks, or unwittingly taken unnecessary risks.'

On 13 September 2007, Environment Minister Lindy Nelson-Carr was replaced by the Member for Hervey Bay, Andrew McNamara, as the political face of the Environmental Protection Agency. McNamara was sworn in as the Minister for Sustainability, Climate Change and Innovation, a new portfolio that had many people scratching their heads and wondering what that long-winded title had to do with crocodiles.

In March 2008, yet another crocodile management plan took effect. It created a backlash of public criticism before the ink had dried. A particularly contentious issue was the direction for wildlife officers to remove only crocodiles two metres or more in length from human habitats. The Management Program plan reads: 'All crocodiles two metres or greater in length will be automatically targeted for removal from defined urban zones unless the crocodiles are clearly only passing through the zone or are in well-known crocodile habitat areas within that zone.'

Talkback radio, television bulletins and newspaper letters to the editor were swamped with a common theme, that *all* crocodiles should be removed, regardless of size. A one-metre crocodile, it was repeatedly pointed out, could seriously injure, or even kill, a small child.

Member for Hinchinbrook, Andrew Cripps, stated 'bureaucratic red tape' had strangled commonsense. He agreed with the opinion that crocodiles less than two metres posed dangerous threats to children, as well as tourists not familiar with the north Queensland environment. 'There should not be a set of criteria that crocodiles have to meet before they are removed,' he said.

Andrew McNamara countered that the new plan did not mean crocodiles smaller than two metres were not dangerous, but would have to be assessed as 'problem crocodiles' before they were removed. 'The Queensland Parks and Wildlife Service will monitor their behaviour and they certainly do a good job,' he said.

But Warren Entsch said his knowledge of crocodiles had taught him that young crocodiles instinctively seek out new territory to establish themselves and inevitabley end up in human habitats where they pose an obvious risk. 'No one has ever devised a plan to safely teach crocs to cohabit with people,' he said. 'They just don't mix. They see us as food from an early age and if they're hungry they'll eat us. They can't be taught not to. It doesn't matter how small they are, they should be removed.'

YOU'VE BEEN WARNED . . .

The entire region of northern Australia is the kingdom of estuarine crocodiles and they roam the waterways of the land, and the coastline, from east to west, with relative freedom from their former enemy—men with guns. The shooters' era has entered the pages of history, and now the crocodiles have their territory back, and with that freedom they have become bolder as they encroach further into the cities and towns of north Queensland and the Northern Territory. They are protected and they are here to stay.

Humans have only one course of action to ensure their safety in the land of the savage croc. Do not assume there is not a crocodile lurking in the water. It is strictly a case of enter the water at your peril.